NO MERCY FROM THE
JAPANESE

This book is dedicated to my good friend Mick Shiels,
without whose help I would not be
alive today to tell my story,
and to Hugh Lowry,
both gallant Surreys

NO MERCY FROM THE
JAPANESE

A Survivor's Account of the
Burma Railway
and the Hell Ships

JOHN WYATT
&
CECIL LOWRY

Pen & Sword
MILITARY

First published in Great Britain in 2008
By Pen and Sword Military
an imprint of
Pen and Sword Books Ltd
47 Church Street
Barnsley
South Yorkshire S70 2AS

Copyright © John Wyatt & Cecil Lowry, 2008

ISBN 978 1 84415 853 9

Typeset by Sylvia Menzies-Earl, Pen & Sword Books

Printed and bound in England
by CPI UK

Pen and Sword Books Ltd incorporates the imprints of
Pen and Sword Aviation, Pen and Sword Maritime, Pen and Sword Military,
Wharncliffe Local History, Pen and Sword Select,
Pen and Sword Military Classics and Leo Cooper.

For a complete list of Pen and Sword titles please contact
Pen and Sword Books Limited
47 Church Street, Barnsley, South Yorkshire, S70 2AS, England
E-mail: enquiries@pen-and-sword.co.uk
Website: www.pen-and-sword.co.uk

Contents

Acknowledgements

from John Wyatt

It is always very difficult to acknowledge and thank all those people who help in the putting together of a book, but I will make an attempt to do so. I do apologise to those of you who I have missed out, but I am sure you will be as happy as I am that my memories have been laid down for future generations to read, even if I neglect to mention you by name.

I must of course start with my co-author Cecil Lowry. I was very wary of this young man when he first called me and started enquiring as to whether I knew his dad, Hugh Lowry, during those dark days out in Malaya and later on the Thai-Burma railway. I racked my brains but no Hugh Lowry sprang out at me, even though his name is in the roll of honour of the East Surrey Regiment. Cecil was disappointed as there are very few East Surreys left alive today, but nevertheless he asked if he could come down to Sydenham and talk to me about my experiences.

We spent a pleasant afternoon together chatting about the Malayan campaign, the Burma/Thai railway and my experiences in Japan. I showed him some of my photographs and newspaper cuttings and told him my story briefly.

'John, this is one of the most amazing stories I have ever heard. Have you considered putting it down in book form,' he said.

Initially I was very reluctant as I have always kept my experiences at the hands of the Japanese quiet (only telling my close family and friends), but Cecil was so persuasive that I agreed he could help me write this book. As I have grown older and seen many of my colleagues pass away, I felt that perhaps it was time for me to tell my story, in order that future generations know just what we went through defending the British Empire with the 'Forgotten Army'. Cecil and I shed a few tears for his father and the rest of the East

Surreys who are no longer with us – thank you Cecil for persuading me to put my story down in print.

For a returning POW, probably the most important people in their lives were their families. I want to thank my mother and father, Laura and James, along with my brothers Jim and George, and my sister Doreen for their help and support during those difficult days in the aftermath of the war. Without their support it would have been even more difficult for me to get back into a civilised society, and I don't think I would have made it this far to tell my story.

Of course thanks are very much due to my immediate family, my wife Molly and daughters Janet and Jane, for putting up with my moods and tantrums during the past sixty-three years.

I am deeply grateful for help given to me by my good friend Peter Bruton. I first came across Peter when he was researching the Alexandra Hospital Massacre, as his Uncle, John Bruton, had been killed there. I was able to help him with his research and of course his material has provided me with back-up for this book.

I would like to thank Roger Mansell of the Centre for Research into Allied POWs under the Japanese, for providing me with a great deal of information about the two camps in Japan. Keith Andrews for his help in obtaining information from original POW cards. I would also like to thank the National Archives at Kew, the Imperial War Museum, the Surrey History Centre at Woking, the East Surrey Museum at Clandon, the Manchester Regiment Museum at Ashton-Under-Lyne and Simon Parkin of Cheadle Hulme School.

John Wyatt
October 2008

Prologue

The one-armed bandit strode into the hut and said to us in broken English: 'All waru pinish, u men to Englando.' He was closely followed by a Japanese interpreter who calmly informed us that two huge bombs had been dropped, killing many Japanese people: the Imperial Japanese Army had surrendered and we were free to return home.

'It is very bad,' he said. 'Japan is appealing to the United Nations.'

He promptly turned his back on us and walked out to much cheering and laughter.

After nearly four years of hell it dawned on me that perhaps I might just see my family again, yet I was fearful of such a thought; times had been so tough over the past three and a half years that a violent and painful death still seemed inevitable. My hopes of survival had been dashed so many times that I simply refused to believe these men for whom I held such hate.

An American doctor came in soon after and said:

'Men, your freedom is here. You have suffered much but I beg of you all, do not go out looking for revenge; one bullet or bayonet through you and all the horrors you have suffered will be in vain.'

Somehow suddenly the air in the hut became fresher and cleaner than it really was and at this point many of us knelt down to pray. Others were shouting, some were crying, some didn't move at all and the lads who were too weak to move just lay there staring up at the ceiling. We were going home.

It is now more than sixty-three years since the Japanese commander of Nagoya Number Nine Camp made his farewell speech to us on 3 September 1945. For most of the past sixty-three years I have tried to blank out those awful memories, but like most of my colleagues still alive it has been impossible to do so. For many years it was extremely difficult for me to speak about my experiences, but as I reach the twilight of my life and watch my grandchildren grow into adulthood, I feel that the time has come to share my story.

Chapter 1

It All Begins

Things had just about settled down in the United Kingdom after the horrors of the First World War when I entered the world on 21 January 1920.

My father had served in the Royal Navy prior to the First World War, and was awarded the Sea Gallantry Medal in 1911 whilst serving on the cruiser HMS *Duke of Edinburgh*. On 13 December just off Gibraltar, the *Edinburgh* received a mayday call for assistance from the SS *Delhi*, in trouble just a few miles away. Dad and his crew put to sea in their lifeboat and brought many of the crew back to safety. Mum told me that it was a proud moment for the family when King George presented him with his medal at Buckingham Palace.

The Wyatt family lived in Sydenham, south London and as I grew up there during the nineteen twenties and early thirties life was very enjoyable, despite the fact that money was short and we could only afford the basics. I spent many happy hours as a youngster out in the fresh air playing with my brothers Jim and George and my sister Doreen, in the local parks. We would often play at being soldiers fighting imaginary armies amongst the trees. Little did I know that, ten years later, such games would turn into horrific reality in the jungles of Malaya.

My mother was a staunch Catholic, and at the age of seven I started at the local Catholic school about half a mile from our house in Madden Road, where Miss Murphy was 'in charge'. Although dad was out of work for long periods at that time he did not sign on the dole, but earned a crust by taking bets illegally for the local bookie Fred Delahory. Fred had a general store near us that he used as a cover for his bookmaking activities. Dad would go round the houses taking bets for Fred and was often pursued by the police, who would dress up as road workers to try and catch him red-handed. One day I remember them chasing him through our kitchen whilst we were having dinner; Dad ran out through the back door, jumped the fence into next door's garden and came out of their front door to make his escape. He was often arrested and frequently spent the night in the cells of the local police station. When he came out the next morning he would carry on as normal, and often said to me: 'Johnny, here's a penny for an apple. Take this cloth bag of bets to the bookies and make sure you get there before two o'clock and hide it under your jersey'.

When my brothers and I became teenagers, my mother managed to get us all jobs in the local Co-operative Society. She had great ambitions for her three sons; a good grounding in this popular movement seemed to her a good way of getting us into a solid career working for the largest chain of stores in England at the time. My eldest brother George was already working there when I joined him in 1935, at the age of fifteen, and George and I had a happy time for the next five years. I began as an errand boy taking deliveries out on a push-bike and gradually worked my way up to be a warehouseman.

The Co-op gave us a fortnight's holiday with pay each year, a real bonus in those times and we would usually go to the local cinema and dances at weekends. We used to chat up girls at the dances and I was just eighteen when I met my first regular girlfriend Elsie. Elsie and I went out together for the next few years, and we both really felt that we would end up getting married. I even gave her a ring that cost me seven shillings and sixpence. It was now 1938 and war clouds were beginning to gather over Europe. It never crossed my young mind that within two years I would be plunged into one of the most horrific conflicts that the world had ever seen.

I was only four months out of my teens in May 1940 when a letter arrived informing me that I had been conscripted and told to report to a little hut just a mile or so away in Penge. Being a navy man, dad wanted me to join the navy but when I arrived at the recruiting office and told the sergeant on the desk that I wanted to join the navy, he just said, 'We'll see what we can do laddie.'

A few weeks later, on 24 June 1940, I received a letter informing me that I was to join the East Surreys and report to Richmond Park - so much for any sort of choice. I've often wondered how different the next five years would have been if I had been called up to the navy instead of the army.

When we arrived at Richmond Park a Lance Corporal greeted us. 'Are you lads happy?' he said.

'Yes Sir,' we chorused, knowing quite well that was the reply he wanted. 'Don't call me sir. It's Corporal from now on,' he barked.

Although I was nervous and quite scared about what might lie ahead, the first six months of my army life was very enjoyable. We were a happy bunch of conscripts together, enjoying the outdoor life as well as the discipline for which the army was renowned. Our days were taken up with drill, route marches and general discipline. We often complained about the petty rules and regulations but little did we know this discipline and fitness would help us endure the horrors that were to come. We were also taught how to strip and rebuild a Bren Gun and to fire the 303 Lee Enfield rifle on a range in Byfleet.

From early September, when the Germans started bombing London, our field training was constantly interrupted by the sound of the air raid sirens: this meant long frustrating mornings (and afternoons) spent in the air raid shelters. There was nothing we could do about it though as the officers ordered us underground as soon as the sirens went off. The evacuation from Dunkirk had taken place in June, and the Germans were now bombing the capital on a regular basis. An invasion was expected at any time and we were often 'standing to' (the army expression for an advanced state of readiness) to be mobilised at a moment's notice.

At the beginning of December 1940 we were informed by the commanding officer that the regiment was to be posted overseas, and that we could take two weeks' embarkation leave. Relaxing at home with my family, my brother Jim called in and said to me: 'I hear you are being posted overseas, John. Why don't you come over to the fire station one day before you leave and meet the boys?'

A few days later I caught the bus over to Perrivale. As I was walking around the station looking for my brother, I heard a soft Irish accent: 'Are you looking for someone?' a woman asked. I told her I was looking for Jim Wyatt: 'Oh, you must be his brother. He's expecting you. My name's Molly,' she said. Jim had already told her that I had been conscripted and she wished me well as Jim led me off on a tour of the station.

On the evening before we were due to leave Kingston Barracks, I went round to see Elsie at her parents' flat. At that time it was not the done thing to go into your girlfriend's house, so Elsie came out to meet me on the doorstep.

'I'm going off tomorrow, Elsie,' I said.

She started to cry. Although I didn't know it, this was the last time I would see Elsie for nearly five years. That moment when we hugged in front of her block of flats was to stay with me through the dark days that followed.

Just before Christmas 1940 we left Kingston Barracks and travelled by open truck up to St. Pancras Station. It was freezing cold and very uncomfortable on the trucks so we were all very glad when they pulled into the station and we could stretch our legs and get our circulation going again. Our destination was top secret and even when we boarded a train bound for Glasgow we were not sure where we were going. Everyone had their own wild theories but it was not until several weeks later that we knew that the Far East was a distinct possibility, as Japan had been making threatening noises towards British possessions in that part of the world for some time. She desperately wanted to expand her empire and the attractive rubber and tin resources of Malaya were likely to be a prime target. (Malaya had more than three million acres of rubber trees and produced over half the world's tin.) The bustling port of Singapore was also thought to be a target for the Japanese and of course we knew that the regulars of the Surreys were already there.

Unfortunately the temperature on the train was not much higher than on the trucks and we were very cold as the carriage crawled up through the dismal English and Scottish countryside. Again it was a relief to disembark and as we marched down the dock, the size of the ship tied up alongside the pier took my breath away. I'd never seen a ship that huge before.

The ship's name was emblazoned on the hull in bold letters – HMS *Empress of Japan*.

The *Empress* was eighteen years old, having been built in 1922 just along the Clyde by Fairfield Shipbuilding, and recently requisitioned as a troopship from the Canadian Transpacific Service. She looked like a real luxury liner to me and I pondered as to whether I could ever afford to cruise on her when the war finished. (She was renamed HMS *Empress of Scotland* eleven months later when Japan entered the war.)

For what seemed like weeks we sat at the dreary Glasgow dockside waiting for a convoy to be formed before we could depart. The officers did their best to keep us busy with games and exercises on the decks and there was plenty of good food available, but it was frustrating not even to be allowed to send letters home in case our whereabouts were leaked to the Germans. Morale was very low, mainly because we were all concerned about the bombing of London and the welfare of our families back down south. The atmosphere worsened when we heard that one of our lads, Bert Irwin from Egham, had learnt that his wife and two children had been killed in a bombing raid on London; Bert was not allowed off the ship and no contact could be made with his relatives, leaving him in a state of shock and despair. By then I had become friendly with a lad called Frank Seymour who was also from Lewisham and we stuck together during the next few months.

Christmas and New Year came and went, before we eventually sailed on 11 January 1941 as part of the largest convoy ever to leave British shores. The sight was incredible as we left the Clyde. It seemed inconceivable that Britain could ever lose a war with this sort of military strength at its disposal.

The next few weeks were very boring as the convoy sailed via Iceland, Newfoundland, the West Indies and Freetown before docking in Cape Town. The captain informed us that we would be staying in South Africa's capital for four days and that we would be able to go ashore each day to do some sightseeing and enjoy the pubs and clubs. The following morning we disembarked and as we strolled into the city centre I really thought that I had landed in another world. The locals were so kind to us, they bought us drinks, meals and we had a wonderful few days swimming, dancing and generally enjoying the South African hospitality. The war in Europe seemed like a million miles away and this respite gave me the opportunity to write to my family for the first time since I'd left home. Any mention of our destination or task was forbidden, although by now we were all well aware that we were heading for the Far East.

On leaving Cape Town the convoy split up in smaller groups and the *Empress of Japan* headed north with several other ships, up the east coast of Africa. We should have sailed straight across the Indian Ocean to Bombay, but our intelligence had been informed that the German battleship *Deutschland* was sailing somewhere out in the Indian Ocean. Thus it was a much safer option for the small fleet to hug the African coast and head for Mombasa instead.

We arrived in Mombasa on the twenty-first of February where we spent three days. It was incredibly hot and it was a great relief to cast off our British winter uniforms and don the new tropical kit with which we'd been issued. But these three days passed all too quickly and soon the ship slipped anchor again and we set off across the Indian Ocean towards Bombay. At Bombay we were once again able to go ashore and visit the markets and nightclubs for eight hours or so, before setting sail again on the last stage of our marathon voyage to Singapore.

Dawn was breaking on 11 March 1941 when we finally approached Kepple Harbour, Singapore, exactly two months to the day after we'd set off from Glasgow. Everyone was up on deck as the ship glided into the harbour, where vessels of all shapes and sizes were moored. Dozens of planes criss-crossed the bright blue sky – this was the 'impregnable fortress' we had heard so much about.

Singapore was a lively, cosmopolitan, bustling city in the early nineteen forties, probably more cosmopolitan and energetic that even London, Calcutta or New York. It really was the first global city of the twentieth century. We were driven in lorries through the city to our temporary camp and as we sped through the streets I was amazed by the sights and sounds all around me. The colours of the tropical flowers in the parks seemed more dazzling than any I had ever seen before; washing hung out on bamboo poles from the windows of hundreds of shanty houses: the smell of fish drying on the pavements assaulted the nostrils and traffic whizzed around at great speed.

Once we had settled into our camp we were given the opportunity to enjoy the shops, clubs and bazaars in the city. Many of the boys took full advantage of the more specific 'hospitality' on offer in the plethora of bars and any thought of the impending war was pushed to the back of our minds as we lapped up the delights of this paradise in the Far East. The 'New World Club' was a particular popular place with many of the boys, but with the memory of Elsie still fresh in my mind (not to mention my good Catholic upbringing) I did not partake of the 'delights' on offer. Besides there was more than enough outside the club to dazzle the senses; Singapore was bright and warm, the air smelt of fresh fruit and the locals were very friendly towards the newly arrived British troops. I was totally overwhelmed by this city of stunning contrasts as I walked through the teeming streets. Chinese families ate their rice dishes on the pavement with chopsticks and I was fascinated by the way they were able to scoop up the grains of rice with a couple of thin bits of stick – the first time I had ever seen chopsticks. In the spring of 1941 Singapore was *the* place to be, as Noel Barber suggested in his book *Sinister Twilight*: 'In those happy days Singapore was the last resort of yesterday in the world of tomorrow.'

Of course there was a more serious reason we had been posted to this 'heavenly' city. We were all still very well aware that our potential enemy was the Japanese, who had been quickly moving into most of South East Asia and had already taken French Indo-China and Manchuria. The situation in Malaya and Singapore was very tense despite the outward appearance of relaxation and fun.

Our regiment were not in Singapore when we arrived, as they had been transferred up to North Malaya a month or so earlier. They were encamped near the small town of Alor Star and the next day we would be heading north to join them. The Surreys had been in Singapore for over six months, having arrived there on 3 September 1940 after their spell in Shanghai where they had been protecting the British perimeter of the international settlement. For the first time since we left Britain, there was sense of real purpose to our long voyage half way round the world and I could feel the tension begin to rise as we prepared for the journey north into Malaya.

Chapter 2

Malaya and the Japanese Invasion

Our unit, comprising of 180 other ranks and seven officers left Singapore on 12 March in an old wooden 'Federated Malay States' train. The journey north was uneventful and the scenery stunning, but as we joked and laughed I was concerned about what was likely to come and what life would be like in north Malaya as we prepared to defend the peninsula.

Twenty four hours later we arrived at the Surrey's camp near a village called Tanjon Pauh, about twelve miles north of Alor Star and about seven miles from the Thai border. The defence of this area was thought to be vital for the defence of Malaya, should the Japanese invade through Thailand or directly into Malaya itself.

With Britain under threat from an invasion by Hitler's Nazis, most of the British armed forces were based back at home, leaving the defence of Malaya mainly to the Indian Army and the Ausralian Imperial Force, mirroring a similar situation during the First World War when the defence of Britain's overseas possessions was handed over to the Indians. Our regiment was attached to the 6 Indian Infantry Brigade along with 1/8 and 2/16 Punjab Regiments, under the leadership of Brigadier William O. Lay. Six Brigade in turn was part of 11 Indian Division, headed by Major General D.M. Murray Lyon. The only other two British Infantry Regiments in Malaya at the time were 1 Leicesters and the Argyll and Sutherland Highlanders.

When we arrived at camp and the regulars saw our pale skins and lack of tattoos, they teased us mercilessly: 'You lads need to get some tattoos,' they said, and directed us towards the local 'tattooist' – a Malay with a Fez on, sitting cross-legged outside a hut. He had a couple of halved coconut shells on his lap containing red and blue dyes and what looked like a dart in his right hand. The man was extremely friendly and spoke excellent English, and soon it was my turn to be tattooed. It was customary to have 'mum' or 'dad' or your wife's name on your arm, but I decided to have Elsie's name tattooed below a pair of hands shaking.

As the painful tattooing process continued he chatted away amiably.

'What part of London are you from?'

'Lewisham,' I replied.

'I was a student there. Has it been badly bombed?'

'Oh yes, the docks have been badly hit,' I said.

I went on rather naively to tell him about the great damage done to other parts of London. He quizzed the other lads too as they sat through this painful process, and it was not until later (when the Military Police swooped on him) that we discovered he was a spy working for the Japanese.

It was extremely hot in North Malaya, and the reality of fighting in an equatorial climate soon hit me. Our real jungle training began in earnest and we marched up to thirty miles a day, with combat exercises in the swamps and paddy fields thrown in for good measure. It really was an exhausting and debilitating time. Quite a few of the lads took ill during training, often from snake bites or from the effects of leeches that managed to get in under our puttees. I remember Frank Seymour getting bitten by a python and I ended up in hospital in Ipoh for three weeks with swollen legs and severe cramps.

Our camp, originally built to house an Indian unit, was in a rubber plantation in the middle of the jungle surrounded by swamps. It was made up of long rows of wooden huts built on stilts and had no electric light. It was dark, hot and humid and the foliage of the rubber trees made it very gloomy, but we soon settled in and enjoyed the billiard and table tennis tables, darts and other indoor games that had been provided. Some of us went down to the RAF football pitch at Kepala Bata and played games against other regiments.

A rest camp had been set up on the Island of Penang just off the west coast of Malaya, and from mid March groups of about sixty men were sent down there for some 'rest and relaxation' on a rotation basis. Penang was the oldest British settlement in Malaya, founded in 1769, and was one of the first holiday resorts for the expatriates, who used it to get away from the energy sapping heat of central Malaya for a few days. The food and accommodation was excellent, and whilst we were there it seemed as though the looming war was just a distant figment of someone else's imagination. It was great to get out of the jungle and spend a week relaxing on the beach – a great tonic for us after the rigours of training in intense tropical heat.

On 29 July the Commanding Officer received information from Singapore that the international situation was deteriorating and we were instructed to take certain precautions within the battalion, including an increase in the tempo of our training. The Japanese threat could turn out to be a reality and an invasion of Malaya was highly likely in the not too distant future. It was expected that they might try to land on the south east coast of Thailand before pushing south west across the border into Malaya, and then down the west coast through the capital Kuala Lumpur and eventually into Singapore itself. It was to be our job to stop them in their tracks and we were given endless talks by Intelligence Officers about the way the Japanese might fight, including possible use of gas and firecrackers to try to frighten us.

The main road and railway line from the Thai border ran past the town of Jitra just a few miles north of our camp, and it was here, in early August, that we were set to work preparing a defence line some thirty-five miles wide, just to the north of the town. After completing the defence lines, we were given the role of the enemy in a mock attack against the rest of the brigade positions at Jitra. It felt good to get a real feel for combat and it gave us some experience of what was likely to come. As it turned out, this exercise was almost identical to the real invasion of Malaya by the Japanese just a couple of months later.

The regulars were just 'itching' to get at the Japanese after the humiliating experiences they had endured a few months previously in Shanghai. Our Quartermaster Captain Gingell said to us at the time:

'I have seen a great deal of the squint-eyed looking devils and I say without fear of contradiction, that no British Battalion is fitter in every department and more anxious to come to grips with the enemy than the second Battalion the East Surrey Regiment which is not only a very efficient unit (and considered by higher authority as such) but a most happy one, which goes a long way especially in war, to achieve its end.'

As is usual in military circles, rumours and counter rumours were rife. Someone said that the Navy were sending two of their best warships, the battleship the HMS *Prince of Wales* and the battle cruiser the HMS *Repulse*, to the South China Sea to head off any invasion by the Japanese. Whilst we had no way of knowing if this was true, it gave us a bit of a boost as it was well known that the *Prince of Wales* and the *Repulse* were two of the best fighting ships in the world. This rumour indeed proved to be true as the two great ships arrived in Kepple Harbour on 2 December 1941 with four escort destroyers. This fleet should have also contained the new aircraft carrier HMS *Indomitable*, but unfortunately it had run aground off Kingston Harbour in the West Indies a few weeks earlier. The significance of the loss of *Indomitable* was very important as later events were to prove.

As November drew to a close, tension began to rise amongst the lads as we were put on twenty-four hours notice for operation 'MATADOR.' MATADOR was the code name for a push north-east across the border into Thailand using an armoured train with motorised columns, Bren gun carriers and armoured cars, along with artillery and field company units. Our first target was to take the strategic railway junction of Haadyai and then push on towards the beaches of Singora and Patani. It was assumed that the enemy would land somewhere on the east coast of Thailand, probably near these beaches, and it was to be the responsibility of MATADOR to be waiting for them and hopefully destroy them before they were able to set up a beachhead.

Murray-Lyon was in favour of MATADOR because he was not happy about our chances of hanging onto the area around Jitra. Two roads converged from the north at Jitra and we would have to spread our resources across a twelve mile wide strip, leaving us vulnerable to a concerted enemy attack in strength at one point.

The only problem at the time was that Thailand was still theoretically neutral and the Churchill Government was reluctant to cause an international incident by launching MATADOR as it could be seen as an act of aggression; an invasion of Thailand by the British would consequently give the Japanese international support for their aggression in Asia. Churchill had to be certain that the Japanese had an invasion force heading for Thailand if MATADOR was to be launched.

On 6 December tension began to rise even more as reports of a large Japanese force in the Gulf of Siam began to filter through; within half an hour we were in our allocated positions at Tanjong Pauh ready to move off, but the order never came and for two boring and miserable days we sat in the heavy rain on full alert waiting to launch MATADOR.

As I sat waiting, the first blow had already been struck by the Japanese when one of our Royal Air Force Catalina flying-boats was shot down by fighters over the Gulf of Siam. The crew did not even have time to send out a mayday signal.

At the time we were never told why MATADOR had not been launched, but after the war I found out that Sir Josiah Crosby, the British Minister in Thailand, had sent a telegram on 7 December to Air Chief Marshall Brooke-Popham stating that: 'The British forces should not occupy one inch of Thai territory unless the Japanese go in first'. Crosby thought that Thailand would resist MATADOR as they proclaimed that they were anti-Japanese and were opposed to any foreign power entering their territory; he was not aware at the time however that the Thai Government were in fact pro-Japanese and were working closely with them. Perhaps Crosby's grave misjudgement contributed to the misfortunes of many British, Indian and Australian soldiers over the following months and years.

Shortly after midnight on Sunday, 7 December, the Japanese

landed a large force at Singora and Patani and by sunrise they were flooding south-westwards towards the border town of Betong near Kroh. By now the opportunity to launch MATADOR had well and truly disappeared and the switch from an offensive to a defensive position had a demoralising effect on us. Had we launched MATADOR twenty-four hours earlier I'm sure we would have given the Japanese a warm Surrey welcome as they came ashore, but by now it was too late and all we could do was sit and wait for them to attack us.

As I huddled nervously in my defensive position an order of the day came through from Air Chief Marshal Sir Robert Brooke-Popham, Commander in Chief Far East:

'Japan's action today gives the signal for the Empire's Naval, Army and Air Forces, and those of their allies, to go into action with a common aim and common ideals.

We are ready. We have plenty of warning and our preparations are made and tested. We do not forget at this moment the years of patience and forbearance in which we have borne, with dignity and discipline, the petty insults and insolences inflicted on us by the Japanese in the Far East. We know that those things were only done because Japan thought she could take advantage of our supposed weakness. Now, when Japan has decided to put the matter to a sterner test, she will find out that she had made a grievous mistake.

We are confident our defences are strong and our weapons efficient. Whatever our race, and whether we are now in our native land or have come thousands of miles, we have one aim and one only. It is to defend these shores, to destroy such enemies as may set foot on our soil, and then, finally, to cripple the power of the enemy to endanger our ideals, our possessions and our peace.

What of the enemy? We see before us a Japan drained for years by the exhausting claims of her wanton onslaught on China. We see a Japan whose trade and industry have been so isolated by these years of reckless adventure that, in a mood of desperation, her Government has flung her into war under the delusion that, by stabbing a friendly nation in the back, she can gain her end. Let her look at Italy and what has happened since that nation tried a similar base action.

Let us remember that what we have here in the Far East forms part of the great campaign for the preservation in the world of truth and justice and freedom. Confidence, resolution, enterprise and devotion to the cause must and will inspire every one of us in the fighting services, while from the civilian population, Malay, Chinese, Indian or Burmese, we expect that patience, endurance and serenity which is the great virtue of the East and which will go far to assist the fighting man, to gain final and complete victory.

Although I am disappointed not to have moved into Thailand to meet the Japanese as they landed, I am still confident that we will be able to halt their offensive when they reach our positions.'

By 1300 hrs orders came through for us to return to our defensive positions at Jitra and as we made our way back, thick clouds of black smoke rising high in the sky further south were clearly visible. For over a week I had geared myself up for a push into Thailand and as we neared our defensive positions, I was further demoralised to find the trenches filled with water.

Time was short and we sweated and toiled trying to get our defence lines finalised. For three days we dug weapon pits, laid telephone cables, planted over 1,500 Land and Anti-Tank mines and cleared fields of fire, all in heavy monsoon rains. With tracks just thick muddy morasses, our vehicles had great difficulty moving around so we had to haul ammunition and stores by hand. Trenches had to be re-dug as they quickly filled with water and the sides often caved in under the constant deluge.

We had little or no protection from the elements and nights were spent in our rain soaked uniforms huddled under capes, ready to spring into action at the first sign of an attack. Sentries were posted and patrols were sent out regularly to probe for any sign of enemy infiltration. Our nerves were stretched to the limit as we knew that the Japanese were likely to attack at any moment.

As I sat waiting with the rest of the regiment, news began to filter through that the Japanese had attacked Pearl Harbour without formally declaring war. Things took a turn for the worse when it became known that we had virtually no air support as most of the RAF planes had been destroyed at the airfields of Kepala Batas and Butterworth and those that were left intact had fled south to Singapore.

Morale sank lower still when the *Prince of Wales* and the *Repulse* were sunk by fighter bombers off Kuantan. Unfortunately Admiral Phillips, in charge of the fleet, underestimated the abilities of the Japanese carrier-based fighter bombers and both ships went down with huge loss of Allied sailors' lives.

Major-General Murray Lyon was concerned that we would not have our defensive positions ready by the time the Japanese reached us so he issued orders to the 1/14 Punjabis to proceed several miles north of Jitra to Changlun. They were to attempt to hold the enemy advance as long as possible before retreating back to our defensive lines if and when their positions became untenable. The 2/1 Gurkhas took up a position just outside the village of Asun alongside a small river some eight miles further south of the Punjabis' positions. Both regiments were assisted by 4 Mountain Battery and a section of 2 Anti-Tank Battery.

On the morning of 11 December the Punjabis came under intense pressure from the advancing enemy's 5 Division's vanguard of 5 Reconnaissance Regiment. The battle of Jitra had begun in earnest. Most of the Punjabis had never seen combat before and were soon forced to fall back to just ahead of the Gurkhas positions at Asun. By late afternoon, the soaked and tired troops were attacked in force again. This caused defences to crumble, and complete confusion and panic spread among the Indian soldiers breaking them up as a useful fighting force. Hardly any of them had seen a tank before, let alone knew how to deal with one and when they realised that their Bren guns and rifles were no match for the enemy's heavy tanks, they broke ranks and fled from the scene. They did not have enough anti-tank guns to make any sort of impact on the advancing columns: the torrential deluge making matters even worse as the troops tried to hold back the enemy's fierce advance.

It was now the Gurkhas turn to face the onslaught and although much better trained than the Punjabis, they were quickly overrun in a similar fashion by the ferocity of the attack. Like the Punjabis, they also lacked any sort of anti-tank weapons.

As darkness descended that evening, tension began to rise throughout our defensive positions in Pisang Wood, just north of the town of Jitra, and for the next nine hours I sweated under my cape as the rain poured down incessantly. It must have been around 0300 hrs when we heard that the Leicesters, well dug into their forward positions covering the two main roads into the town, had come under heavy shelling. The Leicestershire boys held firm until daybreak, aided by some of our Bren gun carriers who had been sent forward to assist them. It was still semi-dark when we heard the sound of firing coming from one of our forward platoon posts. The boys thought that they were firing at the advancing soldiers but when Lieutenant Abbott went to investigate, he found that they were actually firing at one of our own patrols trying to find their way back.

As the new day dawned, it emerged that the situation had become totally confused. We hadn't a clue what was going on, as telephone communications had completely broken down, but as yet we still had not seen much of the Japanese troops in our area. It was just a matter of sitting tight and keeping our heads down. The Leicesters and the 2/9 Jats were taking heavy fire up ahead in their forward positions, but although they managed to repulse the attack and inflict heavy losses on the enemy, their situation was becoming very serious.

It turned out to be a nervous day as we huddled in our trenches waiting for the Japanese. By 1600 hrs we heard that the Leicesters were withdrawing from their forward positions as they had taken heavy casualties in a skirmish, not a good sign for morale of the Brigade. The Surrey's B and D Companies moved out from their positions around this time and fell back towards the town of Anak Bukit, four miles north of Alor Star. We moved the short distance to take over B Company's vacated position at Budi.

For the next twelve hours we lay in the trenches dug by B Company and by 0500 hrs on the morning of the thirteenth we were also ordered to fall back towards Anak Bukit, a distance of around fifteen miles. The withdrawal was chaotic and it took us about four hours to reach the town. We trudged through paddy fields, swamps and thick jungle towards a narrow bamboo bridge near Sungai Bata, our only means of crossing the river. Fortunately it was still intact when we got there and we were able to cross it easily. I was by now totally exhausted, soaked to the skin, caked in mud and just wanted to get some sleep.

During the confusion of the retreat, our Commanding Officer, Lieutenant Colonel Swinton, came off the back of a motorcycle ridden by Sergeant Croft and broke his leg. The Colonel had been on a reconnaissance trip to check out the withdrawal route of the regiment at the time, and although in great pain, he took some persuading to leave us. Swinton handed over control of the regiment to Major Dowling and was immediately evacuated back to Singapore.

The withdrawal that night of 6 Indian Infantry Brigade down the single main road was chaotic. Total panic reigned, as Bren gun carriers and lorries loaded with stores and ammunition tore down the narrow road at high speed in a long convoy. Jitra had been a major disaster; the whole of the brigade was demoralised, and I was frustrated that, with the enemy almost in sight, I was denied my first real taste of action. A Japanese force of around 600 had driven back over 2,400 British and Indian forces, killing or capturing around 1,400 men, and taking great quantities of weapons and equipment, for the loss of only 120 of their own men.

Meanwhile B and D Companies were ordered to dig in on the south side of the Bata River near Kampong Budi. Their job was to hold the area enabling the Leicesters to move to new defence positions and the rest of us to proceed on to Anak Bukit.

It was just before daybreak when we arrived at Anak Bukit. I hoped we would get a bit of rest as I was totally exhausted, unfortunately the rest amounted to about half an hour before we were off again towards Alor Star just a few miles distant. It was around 0830 hrs when we eventually stumbled into the town we knew so well from our previous visits. C Company, under the command of Captain Wallis, was short of sixty men, most of whom had been left behind at Anak Bukit due to sheer exhaustion. Alor Star was totally unprepared for defence, but we took up the best available positions along the south bank of the river, covering the bridge and the areas either side. Dozing fitfully as the morning wore on, I was awakened by the sound of our own guns firing at three enemy motorcyclists who were racing across the bridge. Somehow one managed to get across unharmed and away into the countryside behind us, whilst the other two were gunned down. We thought that this was the start of the main enemy attack on the town, so orders were given to blow the bridge, even though many of our own troops were still on the northern side of the river. We only found out later that their main force was still some miles north of the town, again a result of total confusion and lack of decent intelligence. Unfortunately for the Surrey's, Lieutenant Bradley, eight Bren gun carriers and around fifty men were now left stranded on the north side of the river. By now the Japanese were closing in on the town and Lieutenant Bradley had no option but to disarm the carriers and dump them in the river. Whilst they were doing this, the enemy attacked the town in force; Lieutenant Bradley, along with Lieutenants Sear and Cross, grabbed a couple of light machine guns and engaged the attacking troops. This allowed the rest of the unit to cross the river in small boats. Some of the boys were wounded in this skirmish including Sear, Lance Sergeant John Ferris and Private Jack Whittal. Sear later died of his wounds but the rest of the men managed to get across the river safely.

By late afternoon that day, an advance party of enemy troops started firing at us from the far bank of the river and we took some casualties in this engagement. Before the main enemy force had arrived however, we were ordered into a humiliating retreat once more.

Chapter 3

The Battle of Gurun

On the evening of the thirteenth, we began to withdraw from Alor Star southwards under heavy enemy fire. I was very tired as we had virtually no sleep for five days, and had marched for about thirty miles the night before. The compass bearings given to Captain Kerrich proved useless as the terrain was very swampy, and we spent hours weaving back and forward along the few paths we could find. Progress was slow and the heavy mud sapped what remaining strength I had left, and by now we had become completely lost; I just about managed to drag my weary body along, almost falling asleep on my feet.

As we approached a road bridge over the river, mortar bombs began falling around us and a machine gun opened up from the direction of the bridge. We all dived into the clinging mud to get some sort of cover from the onslaught. I was convinced that the Japanese had captured the bridge but Captain Kerrich and Lieutenant Abbott thought that we were actually under attack from friendly fire. Somehow the two officers managed to ascertain that it was indeed friendly fire and were able to make our identity known and to our immense relief, we were allowed to cross the bridge. With communications virtually non existent, such friendly attacks were always likely and we were very lucky not to be wiped out by the defending Indian regiment.

We rested for a short time on the other side of the bridge, but again morale slumped when Captain Kerrich told us that we had only managed to progress three miles from Alor Star. As we rested on the south side of the river, Lieutenant Abbott took a head count and was devastated to find that there were only twelve of us left in A Company. Five of the lads had been killed by our Indian compatriots as we approached the bridge but we had no idea if the rest of the company were dead or had simply got lost during the difficult march. There was little chance for further rest or any sleep however as the enemy were pushing hard down the trunk road towards us, so we set off again towards the town of Gurun where we were to set up a defensive position.

It was around 0400 hrs on the morning of the fourteenth when we finally arrived at Gurun. Fortunately Captain Gingell and his merry men of B Echelon, arrived an hour or so later and prepared a hot stew for us. It was most welcome as we had not eaten a proper meal for two days.

Gurun was supposed to be one of the best natural defence positions in Malaya; it would have been, had the necessary preparation work been done in advance by a fresh division with good reserves, but this certainly did not apply to us as we were all exhausted. There was no respite however as we were ordered to immediately start digging in again. With only twelve of us left, we took up a position astride the main road to cover it and the adjacent railway line. B and C companies were posted to the north of our section, just to the right of the road, with Battalion Headquarters set up a couple of hundred yards to the south in a hut in Gurun village.

It was now late afternoon on 14 December and we were very aware that the enemy were just a matter of a mile or so to the north, where three tanks (along with about a dozen trucks filled with troops) had taken the Gurun/Chepadak crossroads. Just as darkness fell, the Third Cavalry made a counter-attack against the Japanese supported by anti-tank guns, but this failed miserably and they had to fall back. I was stunned to see Indian troops of the 1/8 Punjab running back down the road towards us, and despite the efforts of Lieutenant Abbott to halt them, they carried on running away.

At around 1800 hrs, Brigadier Lay 6 Indian Infantry Brigade Commander ordered us, along with any other troops available, to counter-attack and try to regain the crossroads. Again this failed miserably under intense enemy fire and we withdrew again to our defensive positions at Gurun. After the last five exhausting days and nights without sleep, I was oblivious to the gunfire and shells that were screaming over my head. All I wanted to do was to get my head down and sleep, but digging in was a priority if we were to have any chance of holding the position. Sleep was almost impossible that night as the Japanese continued to probe our positions and by dawn the situation had become serious: they had breached the Sungei Kedah river at Alor Star and were advancing towards us.

Gurun would have been a strong defensive position had we had the time or the energy to prepare it properly, but we were all totally exhausted. My feet were also in a very bad state after marching for miles in soaked and mud-coated boots.

As dawn broke on the fifteenth, the main enemy attack on Gurun started and we came under heavy fire. Captain Kerrich said to us: 'We have got to hold on here lads – each man have a cigarette – have your last smoke before the little buggars reach us.' A few minutes later they came at us down the main road and we began to take casualties. Aircraft were strafing us from overhead and tanks appeared up ahead. We were taking a terrible pummelling. The ground shook violently around us every minute or so, but fortunately we did not take a direct hit and the trench held up. After what seemed like an eternity crouched in that sodden trench, Captain Kerrich shouted, 'You can't do any more lads, run for it.' As he stood up to lead us away he was killed outright by a sniper's bullet. Corporal Bartram was also hit in the leg as he tried to make a run for it and lay groaning near our trench. The unwritten rule was that you couldn't hold up the company by taking someone badly injured with you, so we left him propped up against a palm tree with his bayonet fixed and a full water bottle, waiting for the Japanese to come. Shaking hands with him and saying goodbye was one of the saddest moments of my life. (The corporal did not survive).

Lieutenant Abbot was now the only officer left in the company and he bravely led us through the mud of a rice field whilst bullets screamed over our heads from all directions. Eventually we reached the comparative safety of the jungle where I collapsed in an exhausted heap. As the day wore on, once again things became totally chaotic as the shattered remnants of the Surreys began to withdraw from the shambles of Gurun on foot, along with the 2/9 Gurkhas through an eastern estate road. We stumbled through dense jungle, swamps and rubber plantations with only a vague idea we were going towards Bedong Sungai Lalang. We had virtually no food or water and were incredibly lucky to reach Sungai Petani at around 2200 hrs where lorries were waiting to take us to Bukit Mertajam.

The long overnight journey down the main road in the back of the vehicles was slow and uncomfortable as the drivers had to constantly weave through vehicles and men in complete disarray. There was no traffic control of any kind but eventually we managed to reach St. George's School Taiping just before dark on the sixteenth. After eight days of continual movement and skirmishes the battalion had used up almost all of its first line reinforcements and was left with ten officers and 260 men, out of the thirty-one officers and 760 men who had started the campaign north of Jitra on the seventh. A truly disastrous attrition rate.

Our Battalion Headquarters at Gurun had been overrun and almost everyone killed when, at around 1830 hrs, the Japanese surrounded the building and machine-gunned the flimsy structure at close range. They then burst inside and finished off our officers with bayonets; Captain Hill, Lance Corporal Smith, Captain Bradley, Second Lieutenant Bradford, Captain (Doctor) Thomson, Reverend Rawsthorne and Second Lieutenant Meyers, lost their lives that day. Fortunately, Brigadier Lay had already left the headquarters. Only three officers escaped the massacre; Captain Martin, our Intelligence Officer, was wounded during the first attack but managed to crawl out and make his way to 6 Brigade Headquarters further south: Major Dowling had already left Company Headquarters to go to Brigade Headquarters: fifty-three brave men lost their lives that tragic day. Captain Howard, our adjutant, also escaped with his life leaving headquarters just before the Japanese attack. He recalled his escape so vividly to Cecil over sixty years later when we went to visit him at his home in Guildford:

'I was adjutant of the 2nd Battalion East Surreys during the regiment's time in Malaya. I was attached to Headquarters during our retreat down the Peninsula watching all the front line people. At Jitra we were all mixed up but we got as far as Gurun where we sorted ourselves out and I ended up back in HQ again. My job was to ensure that all four companies had runners linking them with each other and HQ. It is imperative in a mobile war that you had a good system of runners as you cannot have fixed lines. I was sitting in HQ when the companies were out in front waiting to hold off the Japanese. I said to my CO, who was Pat Dowling at the time, 'look I can't sit on my backside in HQ all my life, I need to be up with the boys'. Dowling agreed to send me forward to D Company HQ with an order for Tony Cater to counter-attack at 0430 hrs. Tony's Company at that time was temporarily attached to the 1/8th Punjab.

It must have been around 0100 hrs when I set off up the road towards our forward positions and suddenly I found myself under Japanese fire. Astride the main road on the left hand side was D Company, in the centre was A Company in reserve and on the right hand side C Company commanded by Captain Alistair Hill. I walked up the road but as I passed John Kerrich's company I came under Japanese fire again, fire which was coming straight down the road towards me. I had a runner with me. You don't travel without a runner, that was a silly thing to do. So we got off the road and into a small stream on the left hand side and proceeded on up to D company HQ under Tony Cater. It took me about three hours to reach D company, who were in a defensive position around the area. Just below us was a gunner OP, where a gunner officer was directing the guns which were supporting the battalion. Unfortunately, Major Andrews, CO of the 1/8 Punjabis, decided that it was too dangerous to send D company back to Gurun as he thought that they were already cut off.

I was very tired by then, and Tony sat me down in the bivouac tent and gave me a glass of something or other, and do you know something, I fell asleep. When I awoke I was totally alone. For some reason they had left me asleep as they made their withdrawal just before dawn. I found out later that they had moved out from their positions westwards towards the Yen coastal road to try and link up with the rest of 11 Indian Division.

It was fairly obvious that I was now behind Japanese lines so I managed to crawl away into the jungle and headed in a westerly direction where I knew I would soon hit the coast. I eventually managed to get across to Penang on a small boat.'

My memories of Captain Howard were of a tall, slim man; his uniform was always immaculate with boots and buttons gleaming. He had a reputation as a bit of a 'stickler' for appearance and discipline as Lieutenant Abbott, on his arrival at our camp in Tanjun Pauh recalls in his first meeting with Captain Howard in his book, *And All My War Is Done*:

'We were summoned to the adjutant's quarters that evening. Having taken special care with our dress and appearance, we presented ourselves exactly on time. We filed in, shaking hands with the adjutant as our names were called by the batman. We were directed to seven neatly arranged chairs. The adjutant, a tall, stiff figure in immaculate uniform, stood there, unsmiling, scrutinising each of us in turn.

"From where did you obtain these peculiar ties?" he said in a pained voice. "I don't know what the CO will say. Here all officers wear the regimental tropical tie with informal mess uniform."

A real pendant for regulations, regardless of the situation, was Captain Howard.

It was a relief to get a couple of nights rest in St. George's School but I was still very tired when we set off again in our lorries, this time towards the town of Ipoh some seventy-five miles further south.

We arrived at the Saint Michael's Institution, Ipoh, around midnight on 18 December 1941, where for the first time in twelve days we had a decent rest. I had my first bath since Jitra and we were given some welcome clean clothes. Our uniforms were in a disgusting state with trousers and boots caked in mud: I had to literally cut off my boots to get at my rotten socks. Whilst most of us were allocated new clothing and equipment, there were still not enough weapons available to go around and we had to make the best of what we had. There were not enough Bren guns to make up for the losses of the previous few weeks so we were issued with Lewis and Vickers machine guns instead, and there were not even enough of these to go round – only one gun per section. There were only four three inch mortars per company and ten carriers were allocated to the carrier platoon.

Lack of sleep and food certainly contributed to our defeats at Jitra and Gurun, as our catering staff often struggled to reach us with food at all. The only sleep we got was when we were squatting in the crowded lorries on our way south through the night. The old adage that 'an army marches on its stomach' was certainly true of our situation at that time, as we faced severe shortages of hot food.

Saint Michael's was a large Catholic secondary school, run by Brother Paul and directly opposite the Ipoh playing fields. Being a good Catholic boy, I was delighted to be in the company of the priests, one of whom came round and gave us absolution on an individual basis. The school's bond with the Surreys became so strong that over forty years later we received a very moving letter from the Director of the school who wrote:

> 'I am happy to know that several of you have survived the war years and all I can say about you is that you fought so bravely and gallantly and unselfishly, thank you ever so much and may God bless you all and your families. May I also grant eternal life to all who sacrificed their lives for us and thank you all again. God bless you.'

At Ipoh we were joined by the remnants of 1 Leicesters, who had also taken a beating during the retreat from Jitra, and both regiments were now well below strength. It was decided that because of this, the Surreys and Leicesters would be amalgamated into one regiment to be called the 'British Battalion.' The most senior officer left alive from both regiments was Lieutenant Colonel C.E. Morrison DSO, MC who assumed command of the new battalion with Major R.G.G. Harvey DSO, also of the Leicesters, as his second-in-command. The adjutant was to be Major C.O.N. Wallis of the Surreys, with Captain W.G. Gingell MBE, MM, also of the Surreys, as quartermaster. The new British Battalion now had strength of approximately 790 men and became part of the combined 6/15 Brigade under Brigadier

Garrett. A and B Companies were made up of Leicesters with C and D Companies of Surreys. I was allocated to D Company under the command of Captain W.G. Vickers, who was assisted by Lieutenant Abbott, Second Lieutenant Carter and Second Lieutenant Leage.

At Saint Michael's, for the first time in many weeks, I had the opportunity to write a letter to my parents about the Battle of Gurun which my mother kept safely until I returned home:

'Dec 21-41 L/C J Wyatt

D Coy
British Battalion
Malaya

Dear Mum & Dad & Elsie,

Hope this find you as safe and as well as I am at present. Before I start you will notice that my address is completely changed, also that I think it best that you should all just send me occasional letters as all your letters have not reached me now for over a month and, as things are, they will take a long time to reach me so one now and again to let me know how you all are. Well mum before I start I would like you all to give thanks to God at church for the mercy he has shown not only to me but to the whole battalion. Three times I have just waited for death but with God's help I am still here. I have felt all along that with all your prayers God would keep me safe. I will only give you one instance of it. Ten of us were in a trench in a little native village in the jungle, we were told last man last round for we were surrounded by the Japanese, and they were closing in on all sides, some of the chaps were saying goodbye to each other, and I was really frightened at the thought of dying, but as the minutes dragged on I resigned myself to it then all of a sudden three aircraft came over, was they ours? Was they be buggered, down came the bombs all round us. All we could do as we crouched there was to wait for one to hit us, but that good old trench saved our lives for it rocked and swayed with the impact. About one minute after they flew off, four tanks rumbled up the road, and gave our positions hell. They flung everything at us, grenades, machine guns, but we still crouched in that little trench. We could not return fire for if we showed our heads above the trench the advancing Japs were machine-gunning us. All of a sudden, we heard a shout 'run for it lads', did we run, but the last I saw of the brave officer who said it, I shall never forget him, was him, pistol in hand, pointing at the Japs, holding them off while we got away. I haven't seen him since. Anyway we waded through about a mile of paddy with bullets whistling past all the time, but we reached the jungle and safety, then on to find the British lines. We tramped thirty miles that day living on jungle fruits. The fight started at seven in the morning we reached safety at five at night. Then for sleep, food, clean clothes and a shave, for we had been at the front for eight days without sleep or clean clothes. We have lost everything, the Japs have got everything, all my personal stuff, photos, prayer book everything, but thank God I am still here, most of the battalion reached safety but a lot of poor chaps are still missing, some of my friends too. We are all together now at a big Catholic school, the brothers here are very kind to us. Excuse pencil as this is the first chance I have had to write in a fortnight, so make do with this.

Keep smiling Elsie and I hope to see you next year xxxxxxxx.

Well mum our worries are over we have just been told that we are moving and our job is looting so all our fighting is finished, am I glad. We certainly knocked the old Japs about while we were there, we are miles better than them and we are sorry we won't be able to get another smack at them, I will have to hurry as the candle is burning out. So I will say goodbye for now, Dorrie xxxx Jimmie, George, Mrs Ward, church, rest of family and neighbours so please don't worry, God bless you all and keep you safe.

Your ever loving son

John

xxxxxxxxx

xxxxxx

xxxxx

V

P.S. I shall have a lot to tell you when I get home, as usual Jerry is here with the Japs, German pilots and German N.C.O's. Tell Dorrie that the corporal who wrote to her is missing but safe I think, and my sergeant who wrote to her got shot in the leg and is a prisoner I believe.'

I was really convinced when I wrote that letter home that the horrors of the war were over and that it would be all uphill from that point on until the Japanese were defeated. Little did I know that things were only just beginning for me in this 'war to end all wars'.

Chapter 4

The Battle of Kampar and Return to Singapore

One of our major concerns during this brief respite at Ipoh was the possibility of enemy bombing, as the school was built of red brick and stood out quite conspicuously near to a railway line. Fortunately, no attacks came our way, and we were heartened on 20 and 21 December by the sight of our own planes flying overhead, though we did not know that the RAF were in a bad state, or that we would never see another of our own planes again until we reached Singapore.

It was at Saint Michael's that the Catholic Padre Father Ward gave us all a general absolution as he did not have enough time to hear all our confessions, the first time I ever remember it being given to a group of men.

On the afternoon of the 23rd, we left Ipoh by train for Kampar, about thirty-three miles further south. Lieutenant General A.E. Percival, General Officer Commanding Malaya, had now decided that Kampar provided the next best location for a defence of Southern Malaya. A crag overlooking the town was over 4,000 feet high, and was considered to be a major obstacle to any Japanese advance. With a population of around 70,000 Kampar was the fourth largest town in the state of Perak, and the centre of the state's tin mining and rubber planting area. The Anglo Chinese School in the town was to be our base and HQ for the defence of Kampar and we settled in as best we could in the cramped rooms. We arranged the wooden desks into makeshift beds with our groundsheets spread across them and settled down to prepare for the defence of the town. We were all well aware that the next few days would severely test the limits of our endurance and fighting ability as a newly formed regiment.

Captain Gingell and his men served up a hot and very welcome dinner of chicken and fresh vegetables bought in the Kampar market earlier in the day. This veritable feast was washed down with vast amounts of local beer and as we queued up with our mess tins and mugs ready, the boys were in much better spirits. The old military banter had returned as jokes were passed down the line.

The first evening was quiet. We were briefed for our defence preparations to begin the next morning; we were to take up the most northerly position on the trunk road about a mile from Kampar, where there were three parallel ridges, 'Thompson', 'Green' and 'Cemetery' running down from the high hills to the right of the town. A Company was to defend Thompson's Ridge, B Company Green Ridge, C Company just west of Green Ridge and my company were to help get Battalion HQ ready in the road junction facing the Malay cemetery, where we would remain as back up.

For a week over Christmas, we worked on digging our defensive positions, but we managed to get some decent sleep and good rations, despite the attention of enemy aircraft during the day. The Reverend Short conducted a moving service on Christmas morning, during one of his brief visits to the battalion, and Captain Gingell managed to drum up a wonderful Christmas dinner including turkey with all the trimmings, and some very welcome bottles of beer. The battalion was very lucky to have him as their quartermaster – he was an amazing man. Then on Boxing Day, Captain Howard rejoined us after his sojourn in the jungle after Gurun, but he was almost immediately sent to Kuala Lumpur to join the HQ staff there.

On 29 December, orders came through for us to move forward about five miles up the road towards the Kuala Dipang sector, near the Sungai Kampar Iron Bridge. We were to cover the withdrawal of 12 Indian Brigade fighting further north. When we got close to the bridge we could hear fierce fighting and heavy artillery firing up ahead, and I could clearly see the big iron structure in the distance.

The plan was for us to wait for the Japanese in an ambush position and fire our weapons down the road when they approached. That night and most of the next day was quiet, but by late afternoon on the thirtieth, Japanese tanks and troops approached the bridge and we opened up with everything we had. After only ten minutes of engagement we were ordered to fall back towards our Kampar positions. By now, we were again reduced in strength, when around 100 men had to be evacuated south with malaria, probably contracted during the difficult jungle retreat from Jitra some days earlier.

For most of the day on 31 December, Japanese planes constantly strafed us and mortar and artillery fire began to increase as we huddled in our trenches. As well as shooting at us they dropped propaganda leaflets over our positions to try and demoralise us. With no air cover ourselves, we had to keep our heads down and hope for the best until the attacks ceased. A Company took most of the aerial onslaught and suffered several casualties.

It was not exactly a happy new year for the battalion, but we celebrated the passing of the old year in our trenches as best we could. We wished each other a 'happy new year' and sang *Auld Lang Syne* with gusto, but I was well aware that the start of 1942 was not going to be very enjoyable for all of us.

The Battle of Kampar started properly early on New Year's morning, when the enemy opened up on our forward lines with three inch mortars and heavy machine guns. Perhaps they thought we would all still have a hangover from the previous evening's festivities. Our artillery replied immediately with heavy and accurate power pinning them down but this did not last long as they managed to get onto a hill overlooking our right flank and threatening B Company. At 0800 hrs we were ordered to counter-attack, and managed to drive them back from this dangerous position. For the rest of the day the battalion was subjected to severe mortar fire, mainly aimed at A, B and C Companies. This barrage caused several more casualties, mainly in the weapon pits of A Company near the frontal part of Thompson's Ridge. Captain Thompson and Lieutenant League were both badly wounded around the face and Lieutenant Cave was taken to the rear with severe shell-shock.

As new year's day drew to a close the situation was looking critical as the enemy had gained a foothold on the eastern edge of Green Ridge. They outnumbered us by five to one, and A Company were in grave danger of being overrun, but somehow they managed to hold their position. That night was fairly quiet, but at about 0800 hours next morning, Sergeant Craggs kicked me in the ribs to rouse me with the instruction, 'Fix your bayonets lads we've got to dislodge some of the little bastards who have got a footing on top of Thompson's Ridge.'

As we neared the ridge, the fearless Captain Vickers led the charge up the hill, where many of the boys were cut down by mortar and machine-gun fire. I was just behind the captain, when he shot a Japanese officer carrying a flag. Captain Vickers picked up the colours and shouted to me: 'Corporal, search that officer.' I rolled him over and found a school map with all our positions circled in red ink, which I later handed to Captain Vickers and also a pocket watch, which I kept as a souvenir. It was probably a foolish thing to do as I might have been captured later and God knows what would have happened, but for some reason we went to great lengths to get souvenirs even in combat situations. It probably gave us some sense of reassurance that we had a future beyond this hellish situation we found ourselves in.

We eventually managed to dislodge the enemy from their positions on the ridge, but by now the situation was at stalemate. We were lying on a bit of an incline, and every time I put my arm up, machine-gun bullets would zap over my head; we were well and truly pinned down. I managed to crawl into a trench overlooking the road with some others of my company including Private Pierce – a real joker who was always singing cockney songs. The trench was too small for all of us and I didn't like listening to him anyway, so I moved to another one a few feet away. Seconds later Pierce's singing was silenced by a shell from a Japanese tank that landed right in the middle of the trench, killing several of the boys and badly wounding Pierce. A few of us tried to help the wounded but every time we moved towards the trench we were machine-gunned.

We lay in our trench all day – the heat was unbearable and we had no water for ourselves or the wounded, who were moaning dreadfully. At about 1500 hrs we heard screams and shouts from just up ahead and as I peered over the edge of the trench I saw the chilling sight of hundreds of Sikhs running towards us throwing their weapons away as they ran. They had been ordered to counter-attack but it seems they had decided to run. 'Me no fight Jonnie – me had enough,' they shouted as they ran past us.

As the day wore on, the dead bodies in the adjoining trench began to smell. Pierce was still alive but continually groaning, so Private Holloway and I decided we would try to get him to the field hospital. We found a couple of planks of wood and made a crude stretcher, but every time we tried to get him on it he rolled off. This made his wounds worse and, as the machine-gunning around us was so heavy, we eventually gave up. There was a great temptation to run away but somehow the comradeship of the company held us together and none of us wanted to let our mates down. As darkness fell that evening, we could hear enemy patrols moving around, but somehow they missed us. How, I don't know, as the wounded men were crying for help.

At around 2100 hrs that evening, the Japanese increased their barrage. Every time I tried to move, bullets spattered the ground all around me, and I tried to claw myself into the earth like some sort of insect scrabbling for food. Eventually a runner crawled up to us with orders from Captain Vickers to move out just before midnight and try to get to a safer position. About half an hour before we were due to move out, an enemy patrol appeared and a quick skirmish ensued. On hearing Captain Vickers shouting; 'Down here, lads.' I made a beeline towards his voice and he started leading us out in single file one by one. As I lay waiting for my turn, I could hear the shouts of the remainder of our lads who were trapped in the jungle below, but there was nothing we could do to help them. As we left the area, Captain Vickers turned towards the jungle of Kampar, saluted and said, 'Gentlemen we've left behind some brave lads in that jungle tonight.'

Although we were not aware of it at the time, we had stubbornly held up some of General Tamashita's best troops at the Battle of Kampar. The well trained men of the Japanese 41 Infantry Regiment were given a hard time by the British Battalion and they eventually had to throw a fully trained battle regiment to dislodge us – the equivalent of a British Brigade of three regiments.

After the war, three men of the British Battalion received awards for their bravery that heroic, (and tragic) day near Kampar: Captain Vickers received the Military Cross, Sergeant Major Craggs the Distinguished Service Medal and Private Graves the Military Medal. Private Graves not only led us through the enemy positions, but displayed outstanding courage bringing in wounded men under heavy enemy fire and refusing to be taken back when he himself was wounded. The British Battalion lost forty-two men in the battle. General Percival paid tribute to us in his book, *The War in Malaya* when he wrote:

'The [enemy] attacks were made with all the well-known bravery and disregard of danger of the Japanese soldier. There was the dogged resistance, in spite of heavy losses, by the men of the British Battalion and their supporting artillery. The battle of Kampar had proved that our trained troops, whether they were British or Indian, were superior man for man to the Japanese troops.'

The official history of the 11th Indian Division also pays tribute to the British Battalion's brave stand at Kampar:

'Throughout the two days of heavy fighting every effort of the enemy to force a passage had been frustrated with heavy loss. The battle had been marked by many deeds of outstanding gallantry. The whole brunt of the enemy's attack had been borne by the British Battalion. In the short time between this battalion's organisation and its first battle, Lieutenant-Colonel Morrison had permeated it with an *esprit de corps* second to none. The battalion's spirit may perhaps be discerned from the answer to a questioner who asks a man whether he belonged to the Leicesters or the Surreys. 'Neither,' he replied, 'I belong to the British Battalion.'

As dusk began to fall on 3 January, we wearily made our way on foot out of the deserted town of Kampar in two columns. Some Japanese patrols had infiltrated the town and we were very wary of the threat of snipers. I was relieved when we finally left the town behind and got to the outskirts, but my relief was short-lived as mortars began dropping around the area near a church where our transports were waiting to pick us up. Fortunately no one was hit, and it was around midnight when the fifteen-hundred weight trucks started up and headed south towards Tapah. The road was completely choked, at times vehicles were three abreast and there was no traffic control. Unfortunately, the order had been misunderstood and we fell out of the back of the trucks at a place called Bidor. Any thoughts of hot food and some sleep were quickly dispelled, as we were ordered to march a further five and a half miles to a new defensive position near Bukit Pagah. News had filtered through to us that Major General Brooke Popham, General Officer Commanding South East Asia, had been replaced by General Wavell – not a good sign in the middle of a war, especially when he sent through a dispatch to all commanding officers which said: 'Although ground won by the Japanese in their treacherous attack could not be immediately regained, the tide would eventually turn with inexorable strength against them.' We were well aware that we had been on the back foot since Jitra and that it was unlikely that we would be able to gain any ground back up in North Malaya.

By 0430 hrs, we reached our rendezvous point in a rubber estate just south of Sunkai, having been now allocated to 15 Brigade. This position was a poor one with open flanks vulnerable to fast sweeping attacks by the Japanese, though fortunately, we did not experience any of these for the rest of that day; by dusk we were again ordered to withdraw. The whole of 15 Brigade began to move out at 2130 hrs and we brought up the rear. We were picked up by 2/3 Motor Transport section of the Australian Imperial Force at Slim River and taken south to Tanjong Malin. The Aussies were a great bunch; the driver of our truck produced a bottle of whiskey, which did not last long as it was quickly passed round. They also handed out souvenirs, and I managed to obtain a lovely jade ring, but unfortunately someone stole it later, up on the Thai/Burma railway. We owed a great deal of gratitude to these boys of the AIF MT Company, mainly made up of older men, many of whom had served in World War One.

We reached Tanjong Malin some fifty miles north of Kuala Lumpur, during the early hours of 5 January. We bivouacked just outside the town and got ready to make a determined stand in positions that had been partially prepared. But with an inevitability that we had become used to, we were ordered to move on again to engage a Japanese landing on the west coast in the Rawang area near Kuala Selangor at the mouth of the Sungai Selangor river.

We wearily climbed onto the AIF trucks again that evening, and after another long night drive of nearly seventy miles, took up a position in the Sungai Rambai Socfin rubber and oil estates near Batang Bajuntai just before dawn. The Third Cavalry were covering a large area towards the sea: our role was to deny the Japanese control of the road approaches to the estates and the bridges across the river Sungai Selangor. We relieved a platoon of the Independent Company who reported that the enemy were on a road north of the river but couldn't confirm their strength. The night was quiet and at 0800 hrs the next morning we followed the 3/17 Dogras in an attempt to capture a road junction, but we had to keep our heads well down as the enemy began dropping bombs on us. The attack went to plan, although the Dogras met some opposition and suffered a few casualties, but they managed to secure the position and we took over the T junction on the road.

News filtered through that the enemy had managed to outflank us to the east and we were withdrawn just after dusk to our original position south of Sungai Selangor, where we spent a quiet night. The next day was also quiet as was the following night but by 2300 hrs on the ninth we again withdrew to the small town of Sungei Buloch, twelve miles south of Batu Arang. It was by now a constant withdrawal southwards and we were nearing Kuala Lumpur.

As we withdrew towards the Malayan capital, D Company was tasked with covering a series of bridges and we did not meet up with the rest of the battalion until late afternoon the next day. It had been raining heavily all night and the fields and roads were flooded making movement difficult. There was still no respite, however, as we kept on moving south in the Aussie lorries towards Alor Gajah where we arrived at around midnight on twelfth. The sight of Captain Gingell and his men with hot food ready for us was just wonderful and I tucked into the food with gusto.

The next day passed quietly and by dusk we were ordered to move again towards Kluang and come into divisional reserve. Unfortunately the MT company assigned to move us had run out of petrol so we marched twelve miles before getting picked up and transported to Kluang. By the time we reached the Coronation Rubber plantation and Kampong at Kluang, at around 0830 hrs on 14 January, I was totally exhausted. As we set up camp amongst the rubber trees we were continually harassed by Japanese bombers, fortunately the trees provided us with some camouflage and cover. We were all delighted when Captain Vickers told us that we were to have ten days rest, the first rest period since Ipoh and it was a wonderful feeling to relax in the cool and rather comfortable labour quarters of the estate. Later that day Captain Vickers was sent to hospital and Captain Andrews took over D Company, I was sad to see Captain Vickers leave and I hoped that he would be back with us soon as he was an excellent Company Commander.

During the first two days of our rest period, we were called out several times. This caused some concern but at least we had a chance to relax and build up our strength again. The GOC for Malaya, Major General Lewis Heath visited us at Kluang Johore and gave us some news about other theatres of the war:

'The Germans are being held in Europe. The lads are doing well in the Middle East and I expect you lads to do the same. But please do not damage any rubber trees.' Naturally this caused a great deal of amusement amongst the lads, with our bodies on the line – the preservation of a few trees was the last thing on our minds. He went on to tell us that he was very pleased with the performance of the battalion and for the next three days we were to have complete rest. We were then to have three days 'spring' drills followed by four days full training and then to proceed back to the jungle on the tenth day. But as usual, plans were changed at short notice as news of Japanese landings near Batu Pahat on the coast was received and at 0930 hrs on 16 January we were given one hour's notice to move out to meet this threat. We marched down to Ayer Hitra and were then transferred by truck to Patu Pahat arriving at 1230 hrs.

A and B Company were stationed in Batu Pahat town whilst, under

Captain Andrews, D Company proceeded down to a lighthouse near the jetty to try and engage the Japanese. We took up position astride the lighthouse road but there was no sign of any Japanese in that area. Captain Andrews instructed us to follow him to try and locate the enemy, but after tramping through mangrove swamps and thick jungle for several hours we made no contact. We later learnt that by that time the Japanese had already moved out of the area and into the jungle of Bukit Banang, south of Batu Pahat.

On 17 January we were relieved by the newly arrived 2 Cambridgeshires and returned to our rubber estate near the Ayer Hitam Road where we were visited by the new Divisional Commander, Major General Key. The General talked to us about the forthcoming plan of action, about morale, and then promised us at least ten days rest. This caused guffaws of laughter from the lads as such promises over the past few weeks had always turned out to be false. This promise was no different when after only thirty-six hours, we boarded our lorries and proceeded to Batu Pahat where we took over from the Cambridgeshires. Fortunately we had been well fed by Captain Gingell and his cooks, and had been issued new clothing and weapons: we were all in good spirits. At Bukit Banang we took up a position covering the Ayer Hitam Road in order to try and keep this vital link open.

On 21 January we were moved into the town and the next day advanced towards Ayer Hitam in trucks, with a view to clearing roadblocks set up by the Japanese. There was tension in the air as we approached Ayer Hitam but the place was deserted with several burnt out Bren Carriers of 5 Norfolks and 2 Cambridgeshires littering both sides of the road. The next day we patrolled north towards the river where we discovered some sixty bicycles lying about surrounded by Japanese helmets and maps of the area. The bikes and equipment seemed to have been abandoned and, as we saw no sign of the enemy, we gathered up the bikes and brought them back to our positions just east of the town.

On 25 January a Japanese patrol on bicycles appeared from the direction of Senggrang, just to the south of Kors village, moving north. As we were not expecting the enemy from that direction we could not open fire on them without endangering our own troops, but fortunately they just turned round and fled when they saw us. A Malay Officer who was with us at the time volunteered to follow them on a bicycle. He reported back some time later with the information that there was a large group of enemy troops hidden in a rubber estate just to the south of the town of Lorus.

Just after midnight on 26 January we began to move out of our positions again, covered by the Royal Navy gunboats sitting off Batu Pahat. The arrival of these ships gave us some much needed fresh hope and confidence and, with no enemy opposition, we set off on foot to march to Baharu bypassing the coast road. This turned into a nightmare march with streams and ditches blocking our path. The thick clinging mud made just putting one foot in front of the other a huge effort, but we struggled on eventually reaching Koris around breakfast time. We rested up here for a few hours before setting off on foot again led by Lieutenant Colonel Morrison, who took us off by another route more to the west of the road. As progress was slow the colonel decided that we should split up into three groups and make our own way south to Batu Pahat.

We marched on through the night, stumbling through thick mangrove swamps, often knee deep in muddy streams, but with great enthusiasm and kind words of encouragement Majors Harvey and Wallace kept us going. Although the Japanese were in close proximity we pressed on and eventually reached the Sungei Bata River. Without any means of crossing the river we then moved westwards towards the coast and reached Ponggor just before dawn on 27 January. It was clear to all of us that we were in effect 'cut off' and the only way to reach Singapore from here would be by sea. Fortunately the navy boys were waiting for us a mile or so offshore and one platoon was able to board HMS *Dragonfly* just before dawn. The rest of the battalion were looked after by some navy shore parties who supplied us with food and provisions for the rest of the day. Our positions were in a coconut palm grove only a mile so from the busy main road where the Japanese Imperial Guards division were travelling south, and we expected an attack at any time. They were so close in fact that we could hear the noise of their vehicles as they made their way down the road. Although we had one or two false alarms, fortunately no enemy patrols came our way.

By late afternoon on the twenty-eighth Lieutenant Colonel Morrison prepared to evacuate the rest of the battalion onto the two Navy ships. Commander Clarke Royal Navy was in charge of the operation and he had arranged for as many men as possible to move to the mouth of Sungai Ponggor, where we were to wait for the tide to fall before wading out to a disused junk. The rest of the battalion hid in mangrove swamps nearby.

As darkness fell and the tide began to rise, the navy lads arrived in rubber boats and we waded out to meet them. One of the sailors said to me; 'Jump in soldier' and they rowed us out to the gunboats. As we clambered aboard, a delicious smell of fish and chips and bacon and eggs greeted us, and it was not long before we were tucking into a good old navy breakfast. I managed to get aboard the *Dragonfly* and as soon as we had loaded a full complement of troops, we set sail for Singapore.

It was a great feeling to get cleaned and fed and as I was able to relax for the first time in several weeks. It then dawned on me how near we had been to total annihilation on that treacherous coastline. We certainly owed our lives to the good old 'navy boys' who performed what was in effect a Malayan Dunkirk. Lieutenant Commander Clark's two gunboats were well suited for such an operation. They were 540-650 tons with flat bottoms, triple rudders and a large upper deck for their length; they had a reasonable surface armament of six inch or four inch guns but for anti-aircraft purposes only three machine guns. Asdics (now called sonar) and depth charges completed the picture. They only drew seven feet with a maximum speed of 12 knots and were well suited to the task of getting us away from danger.

Chapter 5

The Battle to Defend Singapore

We docked at Singapore on the morning of 29 January and were immediately taken by trucks to the Biddadari evacuation camp on Serangoon Road, near Biddadari Christian cemetery on the outskirts of the city. Waiting for us there was Quartermaster Captain Gingell and his merry men, along with most of our vehicles. They had just managed to escape before the Senggarang to Rengit Road was cut off by the Japanese, and had driven south through Johore and across the causeway and into Singapore.

Our first task after the rigours of the past few days was to reorganise and get re-equipped with fresh clothes, arms and equipment. There was no shortage of equipment in Singapore at that time, contrary to what many unit commanders said and verified by Captain Gingell when he said to us:

> 'I place on record that there is no shortage of clothing, supplies and equipment. New arms were obtained which consisted of Lewis guns and fair supply of Thompson Sub-machine guns. Small arms ammunition was plentiful and those units that complained of a shortage are entirely to blame as their representatives did not make efforts to obtain same. I say this as I heard of some units who were short in fairness to the RAOC and RASC. I consider it entirely the fault of the unit and not the department who was responsible for providing same.'

Our commanding officer, Lieutenant Colonel Morrison left us at this time to take over temporary command of 15 Indian Infantry Brigade, transferring command of the battalion to Major Harvey. We then had a day's rest before being transported, just before dusk on 31 January, to our new defence positions just east of the Naval Base facing the Straits of Johore and southern Malaya. Much to our surprise, the northern side of the island facing Johore did not seem to be at all prepared for defence and we were immediately set to work preparing coastal defences. What the tens of thousands of troops stationed in Singapore had been doing whilst we were laying our lives on the line fighting down Malaya, I have no idea.

For several days we laboured digging trenches, making weapon pits, filling sandbags and laying barbed wire along the beach in preparation for a Japanese assault. The causeway had been blown up a few days earlier and it felt very much as though we were surrounded and that this 'invincible' island would be invaded at any time. For the moment however, the Japanese were confining their efforts to bombing raids on the island's airfields, harbour, city and military installations.

Two days later things began to look even more ominous when the Royal Navy Base to the west of our sector was evacuated at very short notice and we were given permission to take what we wanted from the large stores. Apparently the staff there had all 'abandoned ship' on 28 January and sailed for Ceylon. It seemed somewhat eerie to wander around this large base, once the pride of the Royal Navy in the Far East and find it completely deserted. We were very angry as we had fought so hard down Malaya only to see an empty base full of stores and equipment waiting for the Japanese to arrive.

On 4 February we were relieved by 5 Norfolks and returned to Biddadari Camp for five days rest. Once again such a luxury was short lived, as within forty-eight hours we were ordered to take up a position on top of a hillock in the Bukit Timah area of the island. The ground on the top of the hillock was so rocky that it was like trying to dig through lumps of iron but we eventually managed to scrape enough away to create a defensive position. Our task was made even more difficult by enemy planes flying overhead, strafing us on a regular basis. They flew in so low that I could even see the grins on the faces of the pilots as they machine-gunned us completely unhindered. We should have had air cover, but the RAF had also completely vanished, leaving us very vulnerable to air attacks. The island was also being bombed from the air on a daily basis and the Japanese artillery were causing a great deal of damage on the ground. This left large parts of the city in ruins and many civilians were killed or injured.

The battalion was now in a pretty dismal mood and I felt really sorry for the boys of 18th Division just out from the United Kingdom with no idea of what it was like to fight in the jungle. We had laid our lives on the line over the past two months trying to hold the enemy in Malaya and it seemed that it would all be for nothing as the Japanese began to increase their pressure on the island.

On 5 February, the empty Naval Base was heavily bombed and when the large oil tanks were hit, thick black smoke blotted out the sun and a fine mist of black oil coated us from head to foot. It was the most intensive air and artillery barrage that I had ever seen. Then, on the sixth, a new order came through from General Wavell that once again caused much amusement among the battle-hardened troops of the British Battalion. He said: 'Stand firm. We are holding the Germans in the Middle East and you have got to stand here and fight and not turn back.' We wondered what he meant when he said 'not turn back' because if we did we would all end up in the sea.

The outlook became even more ominous when General Wavell himself left the island a few days later, and it was at that point I realised Singapore was doomed. Many of the boys had had enough fighting and just wanted to go home to their wives and families, but not for the first time during the campaign, the spirit of the Surreys held together. Although we were all exhausted, we settled down on that hill in Bukit Timah to face the final enemy onslaught and possible extinction.

During the evening of 8 February, the Japanese 5 and 18 Divisions set off in hundreds of small craft to cross the Straights of Johore at the western end; it took them only six minutes to make their first landing on Singapore Island. The first troops hit the beaches around 2100 hrs and within minutes the impregnable fortress of Singapore was no longer impregnable. The next day, 9 February, we were placed under the command of Major General Gordon Bennett's 8th Australian Division. We were ordered to counter a Japanese attack on the west of the island in order to retain the important Bulin–Jurong defence line. At 1900 hrs that same day we set of by motor transport towards a point near the racecourse and close to Bukit Timah village, but because of the choked state of the roads it took us almost five hours and we did not arrive until nearly midnight. From there we marched west through the night to Jurong Road amidst heavy mortar fire, arriving at our allotted positions around 0400 hrs. Our role was to fill a gap that existed between 44 Indian Brigade and the A.I.F. B Company took up a position on the right of the road with C Company to the left and my Company D, held in reserve at Battalion Headquarters near the brickworks. A Company covered the road running to the north and the right flank of the battalion.

That same day, 10 February, General Wavell sent a letter to the senior officers in Singapore penned in his usual inspirational language;

'It is certain that our troops in Singapore outnumber the Japanese troops who have crossed the Straits. We must destroy them. Our whole fighting reputation is at stake and the honour of the British Empire. The Americans have held out in the Bataan Peninsula against far heavier odds. The Russians are turning back the packed strength of the Germans. The Chinese, with almost complete lack of modern equipment, have held the Japanese for about four and a half years. It will be disgraceful if we cannot hold our much boasted Fortress of Singapore against inferior forces. There must be no thought of sparing the troops or civil population. No mercy must be shown in any shape or form. Commanders and senior officers must lead their troops and, if necessary, die with them. There must be no thought of surrender and every unit must fight to the end and in close contact with the enemy.

Please see that the above is brought to the notice of all senior officers and through them to all troops. I look to you and your men to fight to the end and prove that the fighting spirit that won our Empire still exists to defend it.

Signed General Wavell. Commander in Chief South Western Pacific, 10 February 1942.'

Chapter 6

The Alexandra Hospital Massacre

At around 1400 hrs on 10 February 1941, the Japanese attacked us in force but we were able to hold them back for several hours with a series of bayonet attacks. Things were not looking particularly good at this time and it became even worse for me when I took a piece of shrapnel in my shoulder. I was in great pain from the wound and also from a badly seeping ulcer on my leg, all of which left me thoroughly miserable and depressed. One of our officers asked for a volunteer to take me out. There was no shortage of offers and I managed to struggle out along a jungle path helped by Private Nicholls. Within a few minutes we stumbled upon a truck carrying Chinese Communist guerrillas who helped me on board, leaving Nicholls to disappear back into the jungle. The truck then set off in the direction of the Queen Alexandra Hospital in the south-east of the island.

Struggling to the ground from the back of the truck outside the hospital main entrance, I was appalled at the sight that greeted me. Hundreds of injured civilians and soldiers were lying around on the ground and I found it difficult to weave my way through the mass of moaning humanity. I managed to find a doctor just inside the main entrance who told me to go to an upstairs ward, the fact that I was only slightly wounded and was able to walk up the stairs probably saved my life. On the first floor a medical orderly called Corporal Sinclair allocated me a bed, gave me some painkillers and bandaged my throbbing ulcer but he was unable to remove the shrapnel from my shoulder. The corporal was assisted by his beautiful Eurasian wife, the daughter of a wealthy Chinese jeweller.

For the next couple of nights I managed to get some much needed sleep, despite the pain from my shoulder and the constant sound of shells and gunfire coming from the front line just a few miles away. Ironically it was Friday the thirteenth when Japanese mortar bombs began landing just to the rear of the hospital buildings, damaging the chapel and some other outbuildings. It was disconcerting when allied bombs began to land at the same time at the front of the hospital. We felt like the meat in a very nasty explosive sandwich. By early afternoon the shelling increased, and it was decided that the Chief Matron, along with her eight nursing sisters, should leave the hospital for their own safety and head for the docks. Most of the female military were being evacuated from Singapore because of the possibility of Japanese reprisals should the city fall. The commanders took this decision based on reports from Hong Kong about the atrocities committed against nurses from Saint Stephens Hospital. Unfortunately, many of these brave women died later when their ships were sunk shortly after leaving the island.

By now the hospital was crammed with around 800 patients, mainly British, but with some Indians, Malays and Australians. New casualties were arriving by the lorry load every hour – it was just total chaos. Around 200 medical staff of 32 Company Royal Army Medical Corps did a wonderful job under difficult circumstances tending for the badly injured soldiers. Patients were crammed into wards with many left lying on the floor or in camp beds lodged in every nook and cranny of the hospital. Even the dining room had been converted into a temporary ward. One of the biggest problems the hospital faced, along with the lack of space for the wounded, was the lack of water. Much of the mains supply in Singapore had been damaged by the bombing, and supplies were kept in every available container including buckets, baths and petrol cans. The electricity supply had also been cut off and operations were conducted by torch and candlelight. The situation was indeed becoming desperate.

I managed to get some sleep during the night of the thirteenth/

fourteenth, but I was awoken just after 0800 hrs by the noise of heavy bombs landing all around the hospital. The shelling went on for most of the morning and it was just before lunchtime when I hobbled across to the window to see what was happening outside. I was stunned by the sight that met my eyes as I gazed out; Japanese soldiers were advancing across the hospital grounds and seconds later all hell broke out downstairs. They had entered the hospital and gone berserk bayoneting surgeons, nurses and patients – some of whom were still lying in the operating theatres. Doctors tried to plead with the Japanese to show some mercy but their pleas fell on deaf ears as they went about their awful business.

I suddenly remembered that I still had the dead Japanese Officer's watch that I had taken from him back at Kampar. I began to panic. God, I thought, if they find that on me I'm definitely dead! I got out of bed, grabbed the watch, and limped as quickly as I could to the toilet and with great difficulty placed it on top of the cistern, then quickly got back into bed.

With the massacre going on downstairs, Corporal Sinclair was most concerned about what the Japanese might do to his very attractive wife if they found her so he decided to dress her up as a man. As the corporal tried to dress her she clung to him in terror, this made the task difficult but he managed to push her out of the door hoping she might get away. A few minutes later two Japanese soldiers came running up the stairs and burst in through the swing doors. One was over six feet tall and the other was very short, and for a moment they just stood there motionless looking down the ward. Although I was petrified, it was quite amusing to see that one of them held a squawking and wriggling duck under his right arm.

There were five of us in that small ward and after a few seconds the taller one moved to two heavily bandaged soldiers nearest the door and after searching their wrists for watches, proceeded to bayonet both of them to death. My whole body started to go numb and I began to come to terms with fact that I had only a few minutes of my life left. I was certain that they would work their way down the ward killing all of us. Meanwhile Corporal Sinclair stepped towards them with tea and bread on a tray and tried to pacify them. They were having none of it though, and with cries of *'Kurrah, Kurrah'* they knocked him unconscious with heavy blows from their rifle butts. They then dragged him out of the ward and that was the last I saw of that brave corporal. At that point a Japanese officer entered the ward and, on seeing what had happened, screamed and shouted at the two soldiers, then shoved them out of the ward. As he turned to leave he apologised to the three of us left alive and said in English 'I am sorry but my men are tired and hungry – they have been fighting without rest or food for many days.' How this fact explains away the terrible wanton killing of two defenceless men lying injured on their beds I just don't know. These awful inhumane acts were to be my first, but not the last, taste of the Japanese soldiers' blatant disregard for human life, and their hatred for Allied Prisoners of War.

I found out later that Corporal Sinclair and his wife were seen a couple of times, once with their hands tied being marched away and later in the end room at the Sisters' Quarters. Unfortunately neither survived the massacre.

Back in the ward, I was relieved that, at least for the moment, my life had been spared. When I opened my eyes the other two soldiers who had not been bayoneted had disappeared. I have no idea what happened to them but hopefully they escaped from the hospital. The bodies of the two unfortunate lads who had been killed still lay in their beds at the end of the ward. In all the drama of the last few minutes I had forgotten about my injury and as I relaxed I became aware that my ulcer was throbbing: the pain was intense. With no one to dress it I had to do it myself with a bandage and some scissors I found on a medical tray. The ulcer was the size of a half crown (fifty pence piece today) and was a mass of heaving, squirming maggots. I stumbled to the toilets and quickly washed them away, to reveal pink healthy flesh: they had eaten all the dead flesh away.

Recently I was amazed to discover that, even 60 years on, maggots are still used in hospitals to help heal wounds the 'natural way'. In fact Dr David Rogers of Oxford University is leading the way into research on their benefits and it was quite amusing to read him being described as a pioneer in the 'fledgling' field of maggot therapy. I would suggest that our medical officers back in Singapore and up on the Burma–Thai railway were the real pioneers in maggot therapy. 'It's got global appeal. It's ludicrously cost-effective and low-tec,' said Dr John Church, one of Dr Rogers' colleagues. Well many of us back in 1942 can vouch for that Dr Church and we could have told you so.

As I lay on my bed with my eyes firmly closed for what seemed like hours playing dead and giving thanks for my salvation, events in the rest of the hospital were taking a turn for the worse. It was not until many years after the war that I found out that I had the very dubious privilege of being in the Alexandra Military Hospital, Singapore, during what was one of the worst and little known cold-blooded massacres of Allied soldiers during the Second World War. The slaughter that was to follow was compounded by the fact that many of those killed were non-combatant medical staff, several of them women and one Padre. I was not aware of the full story behind the massacre that went on as I lay there until I spoke to my good friend Peter Bruton, in 1989, when he contacted me about my experiences; he was researching what went on in the hospital during those two days because his uncle, Corporal Peter Bruton was one of the medical staff brutally murdered by the Japanese during the raid. I am indebted to Peter for allowing me to outline the events that followed as I remained firmly under my sheets on the first floor ward.

I was probably one of the first people to see the Japanese troops approaching the hospital, led by a soldier carrying a Japanese flag. There were about100 of them advancing across the hospital grounds. As they approached the Sisters' Quarters, Captain Bartlett of the RAMC walked towards them with his arms in the air shouting 'hospital, hospital' and pointing to his red-cross brassard. As he was still wearing his steel helmet, the captain must have looked like a threat to the Japanese who fired at him. Fortunately for him, they missed and he sprinted back into a ward room, closely followed by a grenade which exploded harmlessly against a wall.

The situation for the staff and patients inside the hospital now looked pretty bleak. Lieutenant Colonel Cravan, Commanding Officer of the Hospital, was discussing the gravity of the situation with his officer in charge of Radiography, Major Bull, in an upstairs office when a bullet came in through the open window causing them to throw themselves to the floor. The colonel decided to go downstairs to assess the situation for himself but before he could leave the room, all hell broke out below, with explosions, gunfire and screaming echoing through the corridors. The colonel decided to sit tight for a while, and after about half an hour, when things began to quieten down, he went downstairs with his aides to assess the situation. The scene that greeted him was of utter carnage. More than fifty patients and staff had been shot or bayoneted and many others had been taken away by the Japanese soldiers.

Some of the patients lying on the floor in the dining room saw, through the open doors, soldiers of the Allied 44 Indian Brigade moving swiftly along the corridor from the medical wards, closely followed by a cluster of Japanese troops. Why the Punjabis were fighting in the hospital no one knows, but some people believe that the presence of armed troops in and around the hospital inflamed the situation causing the Japanese to react as they did.

The assault on the hospital was undertaken by a company of about 175 men. They were dressed in full combat kit, consisting of green tropical uniforms, steel helmets, rifles, bayonets and machine guns. They were heavily camouflaged with small branches, twigs and leaves stuck all over their bodies and were dirty and smelly. They also gave the impression of being either drunk or high on drugs. One group came in from the adjacent railway line and quickly entered the hospital through the main entrance. A second group came in through the rear entrance and the patient's dining room: a third entered through the operating rooms' windows and through the surgical wards. Staff in the laboratory saw the first group coming towards the hospital; they tried to escape towards the main building but were tragically cut down by a burst of machine-gun fire. The officer in charge, Major J.A. Calder RAMC, was killed along with Sergeant Williams RAMC but Corporal Saint managed to crawl to the main building with a wounded arm where Private Sutton attended to the wound.

Two of the second group of Japanese soldiers who had pursued the retreating Punjabi soldiers entered the temporary ward in the dining room where over 100 patients were lying on temporary beds. One of the two started beating the helpless patients with a brush whilst the other completely humiliated another by urinating on him. Lieutenant Weston, who was in charge of the reception area, decided to take a white sheet and wave it out of the back door of the hospital, but when the first Japanese soldier reached him he simply bayoneted the defenceless officer through the white flag. The blade entered through his upper chest and out through his lower back. The rest of the soldiers in this group stormed into the room and began shooting and bayoneting many of the helpless patients. Among those killed in this early orgy of violence was Padre Smith of the Gordon Highlanders, Staff Sergeant Walker of the Royal Army Dental Corps and Sergeant Sherriff of the Royal Army Medical Corps.

With the hospital in a complete state of disarray and panic, many people tried to escape from the marauding assassins, some with greater degrees of success than others. Those who tried to escape through the main entrance were simply mown down by rifle and machine-gun fire. Others met their fate in the rear corridor where they were bayoneted or shot before they had a chance to leave the building. Corporal Collins was bayoneted through the chest but fortunately they missed his vital organs and he survived the atrocity. Company Quartermaster Sergeant Hartley was not so fortunate and was the oldest man to die in the massacre, aged fifty-seven.

This group of Japanese soldiers seemed to have completed the worst atrocities. They proceeded to enter the medical wards bayoneting patients and heavily beating up others. They then forced the entire medical staff and the wounded who could walk into the corridor, where they left them standing in sheer terror.

Whilst all this was going on, the surgeons proceeded to carry on with operations, firstly in the theatres, but when this proved too dangerous because of stray bullets, in the corridors, only moving back into the theatres when the firing stopped. Operations proceeded under the most stressful of situations, and the sheer dedication and bravery of the medical staff was of the highest order. The staff became aware that the Japanese were now in the corridors outside the operating theatres and Captain Smiley moved over to the doorway and indicated to the red cross clearly displayed on his armband. He motioned to the Japanese soldiers to come into the theatre to show then that they were not at any risk and that it was indeed simply an operating theatre. One of the soldiers fired at him, but the shot missed and hit Private Lewis in the shoulder. Smiley told the medical team to stand quietly in the centre of the room with their arms in the air leaving the patient on the operating table. The Japanese ordered the group out into the corridor and as they moved down the passage they were attacked viciously with bayonets and rifle butts. The captain took a bayonet thrust to his chest but fortunately he had his metal cigarette case in his pocket and the bayonet was deflected. Others were not so lucky though: Private Rodgers, Captain Parkinson, Corporal McEwan and Lance Corporal Lewis were repeatedly bayoneted and all died almost immediately. Captain Smiley managed to survive the frenzied attack by deflecting the bayonet away from his vital organs, although he was badly wounded in the groin, arm and hand. He stumbled against Private Sutton and they both fell to the ground, pretending to be dead – an act that probably saved both their lives. Captain Smiley was awarded the Military Cross after the war for his actions in the hospital that day.

As this mayhem was going on, the patient on the operating table Corporal Vetch was stabbed to death whilst still under the anaesthetic. Perhaps in some respects one of the 'lucky' ones as he would have been completely unaware of the sheer terror around him.

Whilst Smiley and Sutton lay motionless on the floor they became aware of a large group of patients and medical staff running along the corridor with their arms raised. The Japanese were kicking and beating them with rifle butts as they stumbled along. Other soldiers entered several of the surgical wards and began to systematically beat up the helpless patients, many with fractures and in plaster casts. They took great pleasure in twisting and pulling at the slings holding some of the men's broken legs in the air. In the kitchen adjacent to the surgical wards two of the medical staff, Private Sayer and Private Bruce, were hiding a badly wounded soldier, Private Guillim, when another patient burst into the room bleeding profusely from a bayonet wound. Almost immediately two Japanese soldiers stormed in and shot Private Bruce three times in the abdomen. Private Guillim lay motionless on the floor in a state of abject terror whilst this attack was going on, the two Japanese soldiers standing over him. They must have been convinced he was dead because they left the room soon after, leaving him to crawl back to the main ward.

At about the same time as this was going on a grenade went off in the ward office next door, shattering Regimental Sergeant Major Rideout's hand and arm so badly that it later had to be amputated.

Half an hour after the initial assault on the hospital around fifty staff and patients were dead, with many more lying around in great pain from their wounds. By 1530 hrs a group of over 200 patients and staff were roped together in groups of eight and forced to walk to a piece of open ground about one hundred yards from the main buildings. A second group of around sixty (mainly officers) were taken out to a separate piece of land and roped together. Many of the patients in the first group were walking wounded with arms in plaster, most were in bare feet and with only pyjamas on. Those who had difficulty walking were supported by their comrades and if they fell down they were brutally bayoneted. This large group were then marched alongside the main railway embankment, past the Normanton fuel oil tanks which were on fire and belching huge clouds of black smoke into the hot and humid air. As they stumbled along they also had to endure heavy shell fire from their own artillery causing them to dive for cover in the undergrowth on several occasions. At one point the party were told to stop and rest. They then had all valuables such as rings, watches, pens etc. taken from them and were again subjected to beatings with rifle butts and fists. One man, whose arm was in plaster, had it forced behind his back and re-broken – their brutality knew no bounds. By now the group's rope bindings had tightened in the heat causing them considerable pain and some people's hands began to turn blue.

The building into which they were now forced was part of the old hospital's Sisters' Quarters. It was a red brick two storey house raised above the ground on piles, with a block of outbuildings surrounding a small courtyard. The group were forced into three very small rooms, each with double doors opening directly onto the courtyard. They were crammed so tightly into the rooms that it was impossible for everyone to sit down at the same time. The doors were secured with wooden poles and the windows were nailed closed and shuttered with wood, preventing any daylight entering. There was no ventilation and within minutes the heat became unbearable for the prisoners. Their hands were still tied but they eventually managed to untie each other, enabling them to raise their hands above their heads to allow more space. They were crammed in tighter than battery hens and had to suffer the indignity of relieving themselves on each other: of course the smell soon became appalling. The Japanese made no effort to provide food or drink, even though many of the men had not eaten or drunk anything for many hours. The conditions under which they were held were so inhumane that many of the men became mentally unstable. Many began to shout and scream at the tops of their voices appealing for food and drink. Others just slumped on the floor giving up the will to live.

By now it was late evening and for the rest of the night the prisoners endured the most difficult of situations. One of the officers said that food and water had been promised by 0600 hrs the next morning but the screaming and shouting went on all night. At one point a voice was heard from outside the rooms speaking in perfect English: 'If you keep quiet I will try and get you back to the hospital tomorrow.'

As dawn broke on the fifteenth, several of the men had passed away – at least seven in the central room alone. As the morning wore on with no sign of any food or water, desperation began to set in amongst the prisoners. At around 1100 hrs an officer opened the door of one of the rooms and announced in broken English: 'We are taking you behind the lines – you will get water on the way.' A few minutes later prisoners were taken out in pairs by the guards. Everyone assumed that they were being taken out for a drink until they heard screams and shouts in English from nearby: 'Oh my God – mother – don't – help me.' It dawned on the remaining prisoners that they were being executed; this was confirmed when a Japanese soldier was seen wiping blood from his bayonet with a large piece of cloth.

As the guards worked their way through the rooms removing prisoners in twos, the men in the last room became very distressed.

Photograph of me taken during training at Kingston Upon Thames, in the summer of 1940.

HMS *Empress of Japan/Empress of Scotland*. The troopship I sailed on out of Glasgow in January 1941.

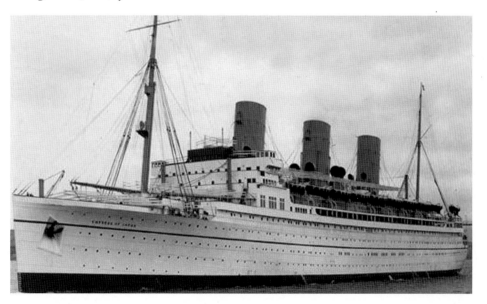

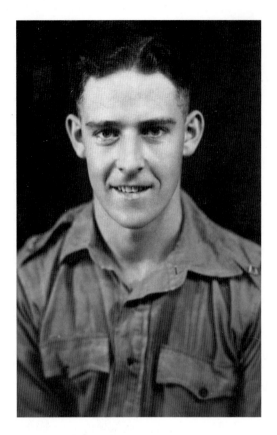

Photograph taken of me in Alor Star in the summer of 1941 well before the Japanese invasion.

The East Surrey 's football team, Alor Star Malaya around October 1941 before hostilities began.

HMS *Dragonfly, t*he gunboat that evacuated us from Ponggor to Singapore on 28 January 1941.

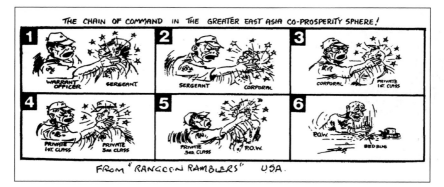

A cartoon drawn by an unknown prisoner which reflects treatment of subordinates.

Card home to family from No. 2 camp, Thailand, January 1944.

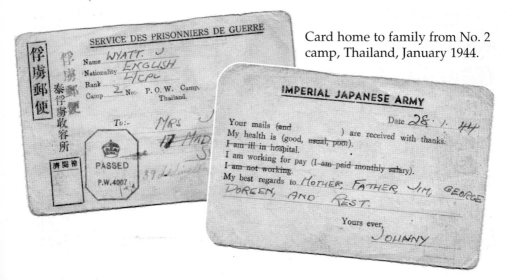

Drawing of the dysentery ward Kanchanaburi Hospital camp, Thailand 1943. No equipment, no drugs – not much hope of surviving. A night scene depicting the departure forever of someone's chum. Painted with human hair, writing ink and Indian ink.

FROM:
Name. WYATT. J.
Nationality. BRITISH
Rank. LANCE/CORPORAL
Camp. Osak P.O.W. Camp, Nippon

To:
MRS. L. WYATT
17 MADDINR
SYDENHAM
LONDO

DEAR MOTHER, AND FATHER,
FIT AND WORKING FEW
LETTERS, RECIEVED, GIVE LOVE TO FAMILY
HOPE TO BE WITH YOU VERY SOON. PLEASE
DON'T WORRY. GOD BLESS YOU ALL
YOURS, LOVE
JOHN.

Card home to family from Osaka P.O.W.
camp, Japan.

便 郵 虜 俘

馬來

See DES PRISONNIERS DE GUERRE

To Mr & Mrs WYATT

17 MADDIN ROAD, SYDE

LONDON, ENGLA

PASSED
P.W. 7882

J. WYATT Nº 6147541 L/CPL

MY DEAREST MOTHER, FATHER, ELSIE
                    I AM PRISONER OF
WAR AM VERY WELL, ALSO BEING TREATED VERY
WELL. BROTHERS AND SISTER ALWAYS IN MY THOUGHTS
PLEASE DONT WORRY. GOD BLESS YOU ALL
                                    JOHN

Another card home to family from No. 2
camp, Thailand.

The ill-fated *Asaka Maru*, the first of the two hellships that I had the misfortune to be
aboard. The *Asaka* ran aground on 15 August 1944 on Formosa.

A painting accurately depicting the conditions at Sonkurai camp. Sonkurai camp was my last camp on the railway and became known as the 'cholera camp' due to the many prisoners who died of this awful disease whilst incarcerated in the camp.

USS *Benevolence*, the American hospital ship that I boarded early September 1945 just off Yokosuka, Japan.

The original *Queen Elizabeth* that took me home from Halifax, Nova Scotia to Southampton the last leg of my voyage from Japan in November 1945.

USS *Admiral Hughes*, the wonderful 22,000 ton American troops ship that took us across the Pacific from Manila to Equimalt, British Columbia during later September/ early October 1945.

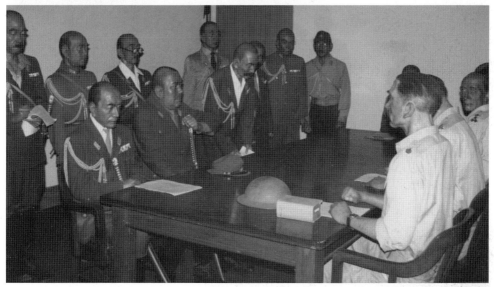

A waxworks model in the Singapore, Sentosa Island Museum, of the signing of the surrender document by Lieutenant General Arthur Percival to General Tomoyuki Yamashita. This ceremony took place on 15 February 1942 in the Ford Motor Company buildings on Bukit Timah Road.

General Tomoyuki Yamashita (The Tiger of Malaya) forcefully demanding that General Percival surrenders unconditionally.

A photograph of Molly and I when we married on 4 August 1946 in Sydenham, the happiest day of my life, along with the day the *Queen Elizabeth* docked in Southampton on 4 December 1945.

My best mate, Mick Shiels taken with his sister and her husband in Dublin sometime in December 1945. Mick is on the left of the three.

To John Wyatt
"My Best Pal."
31 . 12 . 45
From Michael Shiels
Wishing you and
Yours all the Happiness
You Desire.

Several tried to commit suicide – one by cutting his wrists and another by hanging himself. By mid afternoon more than half of the men had been taken from this last room to meet their fate. As all this was going on, heavy fighting was raging all around the buildings and a shell landing nearby blew open the doors and windows, showering the remaining prisoners with dust and rubble. Several were injured by the flying debris but those left were able to make a dash for freedom – some through the broken door and others through the windows. A number managed to get away but most of them were killed by a burst of machine-gun fire from close range.

Among those who escaped through the door and windows were Corporal Bryer, Private Hoskins, Private Gurd, Captain De Warrenne Waller and Corporal Johnson. When Bryer escaped through the doorway he turned left, ran around the rear of the building and ran along Alexandra Road where he bumped into Hoskins. Both men ran along together, zigzagging to avoid enemy fire, but unfortunately Bryer was hit in the back and fell down. 'I'm done for – you go on,' he called out to Hoskins who, realising that if he hesitated he too would be a goner, ran on towards a hut on the other side of the road. Here he came across an Indian family who gave him some water. As the Japanese were in the vicinity he then ran on until finally he reached a patrol of the Beds and Herts who took him to their Company Headquarters and from there back into Singapore city.

Meanwhile Bryer found that he was not too badly wounded and was able to to get up and try to get away from the area. Unfortunately he came across a Japanese patrol that stabbed him four times with their bayonets. Trying to get away from them, one of the stabs went into his ribs and another hit him on the side of his head knocking him into a semi-conscious state. Realising that things were pretty serious for him, Bryer then lay still pretending to be dead and fortunately for him the patrol went away leaving him in a bloody heap. He lay there in his own blood until dusk and as he was not too far from the hospital, stumbled and crawled back to look for help.

Private Gurd had also turned left out of the door and ran across the road and the railway looking for some sort of safety. He saw other figures in pyjamas nearby and, after diving into some waist-high grass, eventually crawled into a drainage ditch where he took a drink of water. (He was just so thirsty and desperate by this time that he was oblivious to the possible consequences of such an action.) As he lay in the ditch he heard someone shouting for help and discovered Captain Brown nearby badly wounded and bleeding profusely from a bullet wound near to the base of his spine. Gurd did what he could to plug the wound and stem the bleeding without much success.

By now darkness had fallen and he made the decision to leave Brown to his fate as there was nothing more he could do for him with the Japanese all around them. He then managed to stumble and crawl for about a mile and a half along the Alexandra Road towards Mount Eccles where he eventually reached the Thye Hong biscuit factory. Fortunately the factory was occupied by Allied troops who tended his wounds and took him back to safety.

Corporal Johnson, one of the other successful escapees from the room, was hit in the ankle as he ran some ten yards along the road and dived into a monsoon drain under heavy fire. He stayed in the drain overnight: the next morning he crawled out onto the road to try to find some way of escape. Unfortunately, he stumbled upon three Japanese soldiers who beat him up badly using rifle butts and boots, all of this despite the fact that it was now 16 February, and Singapore had capitulated. Fortunately for him, a Japanese officer came along and gave him a pass to make his way back down the road to the hospital.

Back at the hospital, the cleaning up operation had begun, hampered by large numbers of very determined Japanese looters resulting in some unpleasant scenes. Many of the patients still in possession of their watches, rings, pens etc. were robbed and much of the hospital's food was stolen. By the time that fateful weekend of 14/15 February 1942 was over, around 250 victims of various nationalities, mainly British, had been murdered. Whatever the reason for these atrocities, the Imperial Japanese Army forfeited its right to claim to be representing a civilised country.

For the next two or three days I stayed in that ward on my own with the bodies of the two soldiers who had been bayoneted for company.

I was terrified as the Japanese were patrolling up and down the corridor outside, and once when I hobbled outside the doors of the ward they pushed me back in at bayonet point. I never got a wink of sleep and existed on some biscuits and stale bread that Corporal Sinclair had left behind. Eventually a couple of Japanese soldiers came in and took the bodies of my two dead comrades away, much to my relief as I was worried that they would soon begin to smell.

The next day I was very relieved when the wonderful Padre Babb came in to see me. He was most reassuring and made me feel as though I might just pull through this terrible ordeal. He told me that the Japanese had allowed us to take over the hospital administration again and that I should not try to escape as he had just seen two brave men shot whilst trying to do so. He told me that he would be conducting a service downstairs later that day and I was welcome to attend if I could make it down the stairs. By now the guards had disappeared, and those of us left were able to move about quite freely.

Lying on my bed in the Alexandra Hospital I began to run over the last few weeks in my mind. I wondered what had become of my colleagues in the Surreys and hoped that they had not lost many more men in the battle to defend the island. I found out later that they had put up stern resistance in the face of strong enemy attacks on a low hill near the junction of Alexandra and Henderson Road, but were unable to stem the inevitable tide of the Japanese invasion of the island. The surrender of Singapore came at 2030 hrs on 15 February, a day that is indelibly etched in the memory of many thousands of Allied soldiers and civilians caught up in the conflict. At least 7,000 civilians died during the previous few days, and with the city in such turmoil, there was no time to bury the dead. Bodies littered the streets and the gardens throughout Singapore City.

General Percival sent a letter to his commanders on that fateful day informing them of the capitulation:

'It has been necessary to give up the struggle, but I want the reason explained to all ranks. The forward troops continue to hold their ground but the essentials of war have run short. In a few days we will have neither petrol nor food. Many types of ammunition are short, and the water supply upon which the vast civilian population and many of the fighting troops are dependent, threatens to fail.

This situation has been brought about partly by being driven off our dumps and partly by hostile air and artillery action. Without these sinews of war we cannot fight on.

I thank all ranks for their efforts throughout this campaign.'

The surrender was probably one of Britain's worst military disasters especially as the Japanese invaders were outnumbered by three to one, a fact clarified by the invading General Officer Commanding of Japanese forces Lieutenant-General Tomoyuki Yamashita in his diary published after the war:

> 'My attack on Singapore was a bluff: a bluff that worked. I had 30,000 men and was outnumbered more than three to one. I knew that if I had to fight long for Singapore I would be beaten. That is why the surrender had to be at once. I was very frightened all the time that the British would discover our numerical weakness and lack of supplies and force me into disastrous street fighting.'

On 17 February the medical officers at the hospital declared that I was fit enough to leave and join the rest of the British POWs in Changi. (After the capitulation the Japanese had the huge problem of what to do with 130,000 captured Allied troops. The only available place to put them was the existing base at Changi in the north-east of the island, where at least some sort of infrastructure was available to cater for them.) As we drove through the streets of Singapore the full impact of the defeat hit me. This once vibrant community was in a state of disarray and confusion and the sight of the Japanese flag flying over Fort Canning was very demoralising. The smell of defeat and utter desolation permeated into my bones and my heart was heavy as I was driven towards what I thought would be the end of my life. There was wreckage and debris strewn everywhere, shops and cafes were boarded up, black smoke from the oil installation drifted overhead and Singapore seemed completely devastated. Japanese soldiers drove round wildly in stolen cars grinning at us, some even demanding watches from weary Allied soldiers. Refusal almost certainly meant a stab from a bayonet or a blow from a rifle butt. It really seemed to be the end of the line for the British military in the Far East.

For the past ten weeks or so I had been trying to kill other people, while trying to stay alive myself and now my mind had to come to terms with the fact that this live or die situation was out of my hands, and that my fate lay with the conquering Japanese. I was convinced that it would be a long time before I would be able to let my family know if I was dead or alive. I was one of 130,000 Allied soldiers taken prisoner: none of us had any idea what was going to happen to us.

Despite the overcrowding and a shortage of food, conditions in Changi camp were reasonably good during the early days of my captivity. The Japanese left us to organise and look after ourselves and in many ways it didn't feel like a prison camp at all, as we were allowed to move around freely within the perimeter. Our officers ran the camp in an organised military way and tried to make our lives as comfortable as possible. The only people who suffered were those who had become very depressed about the defeat, or those with illness or severe injuries which meant that were confined to the camp hospital. I simply didn't realise how fortunate I was to be in Changi at that time as things were to take a turn for the worse some months later, up on that dreadful railway in Thailand.

We set about making the camp as comfortable as possible, drilling boreholes with augers for sanitation, digging latrines and surrounding them with hessian screens. As the weeks dragged by, food became scarce and our mainly rice diet began to take its toll. Most of us spent many an 'unhappy hour' in the latrines with diarrhoea, constipation or dysentery. Naturally the latrines became the focal point of the camp where news and rumours were discussed, and I spent many an hour putting the world to rights whilst sitting on the 'throne'.

About the middle of September 1942, whilst sitting on a hill overlooking Singapore Harbour, I watched the Japanese Fleet putting to sea. Battleships, cruisers, destroyers, aircraft carriers and supply ships cruised out of the anchorage whilst hundreds of aircraft flew overhead. They looked invincible as they went endlessly past. It was rumoured that we were losing the war in Europe; London was still being heavily bombed, most of the Far East had fallen, and the situation was looking bleak for the British Empire. I felt desperately lonely, yearned to see my parents again and was overwhelmed with this dreadful feeling that I would never get back to them or to my beloved Sydenham. London seemed like a million miles away. To make matters worse I had dysentery and my ankles were beginning to swell from the effects of beriberi. I was not alone in my feelings of depression and self-pity. Most of the lads felt that we had let our country down and our pride had been hard hit, even though the Surreys had fought a valiant rearguard action down Malaya - taking severe casualties in the process.

One of the few advantages of Changi was that it was right next to the sea enabling us to go swimming. Swimming was one of the few pleasures we had and it was a blow when, for some reason, the Japanese banned it and put the beaches out of bounds. This was probably my first taste of the illogical Japanese mind. Still, we managed to keep ourselves occupied by organising a variety of sports and entertainment, and indeed these became a very important part of our lives in captivity. Changi already had an open-air cinema which we turned into a theatre, putting on many excellent productions organised by a group of men with experience of the stage from their early days back in the United Kingdom. It was amazing what they were able to produce given the conditions and lack of props. Church services were also held on a regular basis by the various padres, and they were always well attended. It was particularly comforting for me to go to the Catholic services at the small chapel we had constructed. On Easter Sunday we held a Holy Communion service with fermented wine made from berries collected from the trees.

Regimental Sergeant Major Kemp managed to keep most of the Surreys together and I was billeted in a small hut with Spike Shaw and Tommy Marshall. We were permanently hungry and always scrounging for food. One evening Spike and Tom decided to go outside the wire and try to get something to eat.

'Are you coming John?' said Spike.

'I don't think I'll bother Spike, I don't feel too well,' I said.

Tom and Spike left the hut and I settled down on my bed space to try and get some rest. No sooner had I closed my eyes than I heard a loud bang and moments later Tom came running in shaking like a leaf and crying.

'What happened?' I said.

'The Sikh guards have shot Spike and I think he's dead,' he spluttered.

It would have been dangerous for us to go back to check on him as we would have been associated with an escape attempt, so we settled down for the night. I got very little sleep knowing my mate was probably dead.

This incident shook the two of us very badly and dissuaded us from making any further efforts to get outside the wire for food or indeed from harbouring any ideas of escape. Not that we would have had any chance of escape anyway as we were in a part of the world totally dominated by the Japanese: as Europeans we would be instantly recognised before we'd even thought about how to get off the island. You only have to look at a map of the Far East to realise the vast distances involved in trying to reach any country not dominated by the Japanese. Padre Babbe confirmed such dangers when he said to us:

> I plead with you not to try to escape. I've seen several brave men murdered when they were caught. You'll be sold out by somebody along the line.

Some brave men did try to escape from Changi, and later up on the railway, but very few lived to tell the tale. Most died of malnutrition or disease and those who were captured usually suffered executions at the hands of a cruel enemy.

Chapter 7

The Death Railway

For the next year or so we sat around Changi with only boredom and lack of food as our companions. By early 1943, we heard through the grapevine that the Japanese had almost conquered Burma and now had their eyes firmly set on India. The Americans were starting to hit back however and by now they had numerous submarines operating in the Indian Ocean and the South China Sea, causing problems to Japanese shipping as they tried to resupply their troops on the Burma front. It was a long and dangerous route across the South China Sea to Singapore and thence up to Rangoon via the Straits of Malacca; the only safe way for the Japanese to resupply their troops in Burma was overland from Bangkok to Rangoon, but there was not an existing rail link between the two cities, nor were there any decent roads. Most of the country was virgin jungle. There was already a forty mile stretch of railway track running from Bangkok to a small town called Ban Pong, but no track existed to link Ban Pong with the Burmese town of Moulmein some 250 miles northwest. Such a rail link had been considered many years earlier by the Thai and Burmese Governments but had been discounted due to the difficult terrain. Low lying plains to the south, high mountains up to 5,000 feet high and miles of dense tropical jungle would have made the project very difficult.

From as early as April 1942, a couple of months after the fall of Singapore, groups of Allied POWs began to leave Changi on a regular basis for Thailand. As these groups left they were given letters, naturally enough starting with A. It did not take long for the word to spread throughout the camp that the Japanese had started to build this railway deemed impossible years before, and that we were to be their new labour force. On 22 March 1943 we were instructed by our officers to be ready to leave the next morning. They told us that our living and working conditions up in Thailand would be much better than those at Changi, food and medical facilities would be plentiful and that we would all be well cared for. At the time we believed them and were just happy to be getting away from the crowded Changi camp. Little did we know about the horrors we were to face during the following months up in that inhospitable jungle.

Our force was given the letter D, and on the 23rd we were herded onto lorries and driven to Singapore railway station. Sitting at the platform was an antiquated engine, attached to a series of metal cattle trucks around 20 feet long by 7 feet wide and 7 feet in height. We were unceremoniously crammed into these metal boxes, thirty men to each truck, and my basic maths worked out that we had around 5 square feet each (even without kit it would have been a real crush). The trucks had central sliding doors on one side only and I dreaded the thought of the journey that was to come. It took us quite a few minutes to get organised but by sitting on top of our kit we were able to make ourselves as comfortable as possible.

It was late in the afternoon when the train pulled out of Singapore station and crossed the causeway heading north. Before leaving Changi we had been given some tins of bully beef from Red Cross supplies and this is all we had to eat for the next twenty hours until the train pulled into Kuala Lumpur, at around 1400hrs on the twenty-fourth. Sleep had been virtually impossible; none of us could lie down as we were packed so tightly together. The journey had been simply horrific. At Kuala Lumpur we were given a meal of weak stew and rice and very little water. I dreaded getting back into that steel box but after an hour or so we were ordered back on board. At Ipoh we made another brief stop for a small meal of rice, but the main problem now was not food but lack of water – I was constantly thirsty.

The train plodded on at a slow pace through the second night, reaching Bukit Mertajam Jetu around nine o'clock in the morning of the twenty-fifth and then on to Prai, where we were allowed off to stretch our legs. Again we got the obligatory rice and weak stew before moving on again through Alor Star and on towards the Thai border. It was strange to be passing through the point in Malaya where it had all started for the Surreys almost a year earlier, when we had been free men preparing to meet the enemy.

By the third morning, the train steamed across the border into Thailand and we all hoped that we were nearing our final destination. Dysentery cases weren't allowed off often enough and there was excrement everywhere; we simply wallowed in our own (and other people's) shit and piss for four days and nights. It was baking hot during the day and bitterly cold by night, and by now dysentery had got a grip on many of the lads. As each day in those horrific wagons passed we prayed that it was the end of the line and I said a silent prayer when the guards finally shoved us out of the trucks for the last time at Pan Pong, about forty miles west of Bangkok. One thousand miles in a 'train' that was simply hell on earth; at least two of the lads died and we had no option but to toss their bodies out of the doorway without as much as a prayer while the train rattled along northwards.

We were loaded into trucks and driven a short distance to a large open space near the station where we were ordered to form up for inspection. No matter how bad the situation, the British soldier will always lift himself to his full height and form up in rank formation, and although we didn't feel like it, this is what this ragtag group of soldiers did. I for one was going to show the Japanese that no matter how badly they treated me I would remain disciplined and never lose my dignity.

Whilst we stood swaying in the heat on this dusty piece of land, a Japanese General 'inspected' us. What a dismal sight we must have been, but our pride was still intact, and we held our heads high as only the British soldier can. The Japanese General (through his interpreter) then ordered us to pick up our kit and set off marching towards our first camp. The march to the camp was only a couple of miles but by now I was in a state of complete exhaustion and could hardly put one leg in front of the other. I just stumbled in a complete daze along the road.

Ban Pong camp was the first one of many POW camps along the railway I was to 'enjoy' during the next two years. I should make it clear to readers at this point, that the camps often had several different names loosely based around the original Thai name for the village or area. The POWs often gave their own English style names to the camps and it is such names I will use in the following chapters.

Ban Pong camp was aptly named as it stank to high heaven and was a complete hell-hole, just a huge morass of mud due to the monsoon rains. We were herded like a flock of sheep into long huts, built of bamboo with attap roofs, where around 100 of us per hut bedded down for the night on flattened bamboo slats. The huts were alive with bugs and insects of all shapes and sizes. The floor was just a sea of mud and maggots, and cockroaches, ants and spiders crawled out from the cess pits used as latrines into the huts. Large bluebottles hummed and buzzed everywhere – a fertile breeding ground for diseases of all kinds.

I managed to bed down near the middle of the hut next to a man who was shivering and shaking from a bad bout of malaria. His teeth were chattering and he was constantly moaning. Looking around for something to keep him warm I found an old rice sack, wrapped it tightly around him and lay down beside him.

'You'll be OK in the morning mate. Try and get some sleep,' I said to him. He muttered his thanks, curled up into a ball and went to sleep.

It's strange how fate throws people together, but this man (called Mick Shiels) was to become my best mate until the end of our captivity and also back home in the UK. From that moment on, we struck up a great comradeship that was to be of great benefit to both of us during the dark days and nights that lay ahead of us. It was vitally important to have a 'best mate' in a POW camp, as mutual support was essential in your struggle for survival. Many of the POWs who lost their lives in those stinking camps did not have a mate to help them through the many illnesses, injuries and horrors thrown at them.

After a most uncomfortable night, we awoke to discover the true horrors of Ban Pong staging camp. It was awash with foul smelling muddy water and the only fresh water supply available was drawn from a well served by a single bucket on a rope. By now most of my clothes were worn out and I was left with no option but to wear the standard POW G-string. This consisted of a piece of cloth about three feet long brought up between the legs and tied around the waist with a piece of string. It became known to us as 'jap happy' and resembled a large nappy. Our meals were prepared in a dirty, smelly, fly-infested cookhouse and were quite nauseating but by now I was so hungry that I ate anything. Fortunately we were able to buy some additional food from Thai traders who came into the camp selling things like duck eggs, tapioca biscuits and cigarettes.

Ban Pong was the nearest point on the existing Thai railway system to Moulmein in Burma and was the focal point for the start of the new project. We had no idea how long we would be staying in Ban Pong camp, but after just a few days we were ordered to pack up our belongings (not a difficult task) and get prepared to set off on the next stage of our journey north. I was glad when we were herded onto lorries as the thought of having to endure another march was not particularly appealing. We travelled along some very narrow roads for about thirty miles before arriving at an aerodrome just outside the town of Kanchanburi, where the usual row of attap huts awaited us for a brief overnight stop. We were instructed to be up and on parade just before dawn to continue our journey.

The next morning we formed up in the semi-darkness and after the usual roll-call, set off marching across some flat fields towards Kanchanburi. After a couple of miles we halted by the side of the Kwai Noi where we were to await the arrival of barges to take us across the river. It took some time to get us all loaded and transported across the fast flowing river but when we were all across the Japanese lined us up and, with shouts and screams ringing in our ears, we were again on our way. For the first half hour or so we marched in single file along the east bank of the river and then on through wet paddy fields for about four miles before reaching a camp at Chungkai. We bedded down for the night in the usual attap huts and the next morning we discovered that Chungkai was almost as bad as Ban Pong. Though the camp was at least near to the river which gave us a facility to bathe and wash our clothes, and with the proximity of a native Thai village we were able to buy an additional supply of food. Again we had no idea how long we would spend in this camp but we set about trying to turn the awful living conditions into something habitable, constructing a large hospital hut, a church hut, some tennis courts, gardens and a graveyard.

Our job at Chungkai was to cut an embankment for the track out of solid rock and it was here that I got my first taste of what it was like to work the infamous railway. The Japanese split us into working parties and we were set to work each morning clearing rocks from the cutting near the west side of the camp. We toiled ceaselessly under terrible conditions on this infernal embankment, made worse by the heavy monsoon rains that engulfed us each day. These torrential downpours raised the river levels to such a height that it burst its banks on a regular basis, flooding the camp and making conditions intolerable. The muddy water from the river often filled our huts to a depth of up to three feet and on such occasions we were forced to move to the top of a small hill until the waters subsided. During such times many of the boys fell ill and, with around one in three of us unable to work, we struggled to meet the ever increasing workload set by the Japanese. I have no idea of exactly how long we spent in Chunkai camp, but one morning instead of going to work we were ordered to pack up our belongings and form up on the parade ground. We were on our way again to the next camp on the railway.

On the first day out of Chungkai we trekked for six or seven miles, and although that does not seem much, it was a huge effort in the tropical heat over very difficult terrain. Mick was very weak from several bouts of malaria he had picked up at Chungkai and was struggling to keep going but I did my best to encourage him not to give up. I carried his mess tin and rice sack as well as my own and when we stopped to eat I shared my rice with him to try and give him the extra strength he needed to stay alive. Even then Mick had the guts to crack a joke: 'Never mind Johnny, only another 200 miles to the Three Pagoda Pass'. (The Three Pagoda pass was the point on the railway where the line passed into Burma.) From that point on Mick and I made a pact to share everything we got either honestly or dishonestly.

By late afternoon we reached a staging camp on the banks of the

Khwae Noi called Wang Lan. We collapsed exhausted into the cramped huts where a very basic meal of the usual rice had been prepared for us. We were so tired that as soon as it was devoured we settled down to get some much needed sleep. The next morning we were up and away early on the next stage of our journey. We stumbled on through the day in the intense heat and blinding sun: the Japanese guards lead the way and others followed in the rear prodding the stragglers with their bayonets. By mid-afternoon we reached a camp called Wang Takhian on the north bank of the river, where fortunately there was a Thai village nearby enabling us to buy some fruit and other food to supplement our meagre rations. The Japanese were paying us the princely sum of twenty-five cents a day, not a lot, but it did help to keep us alive during the march. We had only walked about eight miles that day but we were all in bad state of exhaustion and malnutrition.

The next day our sorry looking party walked for five miles before finally arriving at a camp called Bankao where we were told that we would be staying for some time. It was a great relief after the constant marching of the last few days that at least we would not have to get up to march at sunrise the following morning. The clearing the Japanese had chosen for the camp was in a beautiful location near a Thai village, with trees and shrubs which would provide us with much needed shade. The sight of the Thais from the village coming over to us with baskets of eggs and other delicacies really lifted our spirits.

'We'll be all right here Johnny,' Mick grinned as he drooled over the baskets of fruit.

For the first few days in Bankao the Japanese allowed us to rest and build up our strength again, but it wasn't long before they set us to work on building a viaduct round a sheer rock face. The work was arduous as we had to break up the rock to make a ledge to carry the railway and when the Japanese produced hammers and chisels for the job, Mick and I feared the worst. Fortunately they had dynamite to break up the rock into smaller pieces but we had to make holes in the rock into which the engineers would insert dynamite. They thought it was a great joke to press the detonator before we had time to get clear, this resulted in many injuries from flying lumps of rock and several POWs were killed in this way. On one occasion Mick and I ran as quick as we could towards a safe spot but they blew the charges before we could get away. The resultant explosion blew shards of rock all over the place and a splinter hit Mick's arm. Blood started pouring out from the injury and as we had no bandages, I put my hand over the wound to staunch the flow of blood. The Japanese in charge told me to take him back to camp and I kept my hand clamped tightly round Mick's arm all the way back. When I took it away it looked like a bat's wing with all the congealed blood and Mick said to me in his usual jovial way, 'You've got some Irish blood on you now, Johnny.' It was backbreaking work and many of the other lads got broken fingers and thumbs as the hammers often slipped off the chisels as we struggled to break up the large bits of solid rock.

Some weeks later and with the viaduct almost complete, we were told to bundle up our belongings and get ready to walk to our next 'holiday camp'. The next day we marched for about twenty-five miles, an arduous trek that took us most of the day, before finally arriving at Tarsao. Mick and I were totally exhausted when we finally lurched into the camp, where fortunately we were not expected to work for a few days and were able to rest and recharge our severely depleted batteries.

After three days without much food we reluctantly set off again to march on into the jungle. We tramped through the clinging jungle for eighteen miles that day, eventually arriving at a camp called Tonchan where we spent the night. The next morning we marched the short distance of seven miles to our next overnight stop at Kannyu South before arriving the following day at Kanyu 3 Camp, where the Australians and Dutch were already hard at work building a bridge over a small river. It seemed that we were destined to be constantly on the move; I found out after the war that D Force was in effect a back-up labour force, hence the fact that we only spent short periods in each camp before being moved on.

At Kanyu 3 we were set to work cutting down trees to be used as supports for a bridge over one of the smaller rivers. The trunks had to be driven into the ground by the crudest methods and as the Japanese were now behind schedule, they drove us harder and harder with the dreaded cries of 'Speedo, Speedo!' or in their pidgin English

'Hurriupo.' One hundred men were lined up on either side of a huge pile driver, holding onto two thick ropes linked to a pulley at the top. On an order we had to pull the ropes to lift the pile driver and then let it go. At the beginning it hardly moved as we were not pulling in unison so the Japanese engineer, Tojo, belted us with a bamboo stick. It's strange how the mind reacts in times of great stress: mine conjured up images of a film I had seen a few years earlier of Egyptian slaves in similar circumstances. Tojo then told us that we had to chant in Japanese *'Iea Go Do'* to keep us pulling as a team. This worked mainly because a cockney lad called Jimmy Kane changed the words to 'Tojo's a bastard, Tojo's a bastard.' This raised our morale and we sung it all the way back to camp at the end of the shift. Tojo had no idea what we were singing and thought that we were praising him, he was so delighted with our efforts that day that he gave us cigarettes. *'Tojo Presento,'* he said with a flourish and beamed broadly at us as if we were all his best mates.

When the large trees were chopped down and trimmed, elephants were used to move the trunks. One morning I was picked out and told by the officer 'you elephant man today'. The elephant would drag the log along with chains and my duty was to follow behind and undo the chains when it reached the allotted point. The elephant would then kneel down and roll the logs into position where they would be used for the bridge. I quite enjoyed this duty as it was not as onerous as others.

After just a few weeks we were on the move again to another camp called Kinsaiyok. It was about eight miles and as the monsoon season was well and truly upon us again, the jungle path was a sea of mud as we marched along. The camp was also a sea of mud and just to get to the latrines we had to wade ankle deep in this cloying, clinging, maggot-infested brown sludge. A whole variety of diseases broke out in this excuse for a camp and it was soon to become a living hell. The latrines were simply long trenches about four feet deep with flattened bamboo slats stretched across. A gap of only two feet separated each 'toilet' seat on which you squatted side by side, back to back, officers and men together. It was a most degrading and horrifying experience to endure. The pits were just a writhing, heaving mass of insects and the stench was so bad that it made your eyes water. The men with dysentery had to sit on these evil 'thrones' sometimes up to twenty times a day. I just thanked God that I had so far been spared the horrors of this terrible condition.

The Japanese had recruited thousands of local Asian labourers to speed up the building of the railway and they suffered more than us. At least we had our medical officers to help with injuries and diseases but they had no help whatsoever. One day, whilst digging the latrine pits, I noticed that the legs of some of the Asians working alongside me were badly ulcerated; in some cases I could see the bare bone through the rotten flesh where flies and bluebottles had been feeding off their ulcers. They were in such a bad way that they just didn't seem to notice the insects at work on their rotten flesh. I made a sign to one of the Asians about it but he just looked down, flicked the flies away and carried on working. It must have been sheer hell for them but they seemed to be oblivious to their evil living conditions.

Several days later when we arrived back at camp from a day's labour, Mick began to shiver violently despite the heat. I was sure that his malaria was coming back so I found an old blanket to cover him up and made him as comfortable as possible. He shivered incessantly and it got so bad that he was unable to work for a week. Each day when I got back from work, I would clean him up, get his rice rations for him and chat to him for the rest of the evening to keep his spirits up. The bond between Mick and I was very strong and we had agreed that if either of us got sick, the other would forego his rice ration until he got better. After about a week Mick's malaria began to subside and he was able to rejoin the work parties.

In Kinsaiok camp we were constantly starving and many POWs died from the dreaded malaria. It was a struggle against the odds just to stay alive and we lost all our sense of decency as we sank to the depths of sub-humanity in these evil conditions. Most of the boys were smokers and even though many were at death's door from malnutrition and disease, they would gladly swap their meagre ration of food for cigarettes each day. As a non-smoker I found this difficult to comprehend but they told me that having a smoke was a good as a meal as it suppressed hunger pangs. I would often swap my ration of cigarettes for the food of a dying man. Looking back, this was a terrible thing to do but it was necessary to do whatever it took to keep yourself alive (this scenario was repeated thousands of times in the camps up and down the railway). I was always very careful not to leave my rice ration unattended for even a few minutes as someone would pinch it; if it was not stolen then the bluebottles would descend on it, making eating it a very risky business.

I have no idea how long we worked at Kinsaiok, but once again we were ordered to pack up our belongings (taking me all of two minutes) and prepare to march to another camp on the railway. I was dreading another long debilitating march but fortunately the next camp called Lin Tin was a mere fourteen miles away – a great relief to all of us. The sight that greeted us as we marched into Lin Tin camp turned my stomach. It was another filthy hell-hole where around 500 POWs, many of them Dutch, were already living and working in foul and dangerous conditions. As we settled down in the dirty huts we soon discovered that we were not the only inhabitants in the camp, we were to share our living accommodation with hordes of large red ants – many of them up to an inch in length.

Our job at Lin Tin was to clear trees from the proposed route of the railway and as we advanced up the line route of the railway clearing trees each day, we got further and further away from the camp. One day, as we arrived at a jungle clearing, I was met with one of the most awful sights I had ever seen. A fellow POW was sitting under a tree staring into space as if in trance. But it was not his face that made me shudder – it was the size of his testicles: they were as big as grapefruits. The worst case of beriberi or 'Changi Balls' as we nicknamed it, I had ever seen. A bucket was placed in front of him to catch the drips and even today, more than sixty years later, I still carry this awful picture of the poor man around in my mind.

Up to now my guardian angel had looked after me as far as catching any diseases were concerned, but one day, whilst out on a working party, I suddenly began to shiver despite the heat. I found it difficult to keep up with the work and got a bash round the head from a Japanese guard. Mick, always fearless, went up to the guard, looked him in the eyes and said, 'My friend, *bioki*' (a Japanese word for sick).

'Ok Ga, take him bak campo, all hurrio. POWS no good ka,' he replied.

It was my turn to get malaria and, as with Mick earlier, it lasted about a week. Mick looked after me every day as I had done for him a few weeks previously. He cleaned me, shared his rice ration with me and chatted to me each evening to keep my spirits up until the fever subsided.

We got one day off work every two weeks at Lin Tin. *Yasume* day, as the Japanese called it. During one *yasume* day a Japanese engineer came into our quarters and asked if anyone was a strong swimmer. He said that they were going to take a boat out on the river to try and catch fish and they wanted a prisoner to swim around collecting fish for them. He said that they intended to drop some dynamite into the river to kill the fish – not the usual style of a Sunday afternoon fishing trip. As Mick was a strong swimmer he volunteered for the job.

'Why did you tell them you were a strong swimmer, Mick? You'll just be wasting part of your valuable rest day,' I said.

'Just wait and see Johnny,' he replied with a wink.

Mick set off with the Japanese down to the river, where they spent some time dynamiting the fish. When the water settled, Mick swam around collecting the dead fish and throwing them into boat until the Japanese decided that they had enough, whereupon they rowed off leaving Mick to collect any dead fish left behind. A little later Mick marched triumphantly back into the camp waving three large fish in front of him.

'These are for you and me, Johnny,' he said. 'Not to be shared with anyone. I had to swim hard to get them.'

That night we cooked the fish over an open fire and ate the lot from head to tail. It was the best meal I'd had for nearly two years and although I felt guilty about eating the fish in front of starving men, Mick said that they all had the chance to volunteer for the job. Once again the will to stay alive superseded all other thoughts in these dreadful camps.

We were soon on the move again, some ten miles further north to our next 'speeedo' camp called Hindato. Here, in groups of four, we were made to dig earth to build an embankment, two digging and filling the sack stretcher and the other two carrying it up the embankment. This primitive means of transporting the earth was made by threading two bamboo poles through the neck of a hessian sack. The Japanese guards drove us on with the usual cries of 'Speedo, buggers no goodo, all men puking.' If we did not work hard enough they would make us kneel down with small strips of bamboo under our knees, and then put a larger strip behind our knees. This meant that we had to kneel upright, because if we sagged it would cut into the back of our legs. If we moved at all they would whack us across our backs with bamboo canes. To make matters worse flies would settle on our faces and if we shook our heads to get rid of them they would give us another whack. One day whilst undergoing this punishment, Tich Maker, a Jewish lad who was kneeling beside me said 'f**k off fly; you might be a POW yourself one day.' We all burst out laughing and got another whack for our troubles. With all the misery and suffering around us it was amazing that we could keep our sense of humour but on many occasions it helped us through a difficult day. By mid-afternoon on that particular day the heat was unbearable. All we had on were our G-strings and with nothing to cover our heads, two hours kneeling in the blazing sun really pushed us to our limits of endurance. I was amazed when a Japanese officer walked up to us, shouted at the guard, and gave us some water. He said in a quiet voice in broken English:

'Me Christian. Am velly solly. You go back campo.'

Some of the guards did have compassion for us but they were few and far between. One of them was friendly towards us and we called him 'Nodder' because he was always nodding his head. He would try to engage us in conversation, which was a bit difficult as he spoke very little English, and was always wanting to know things like where we came from. One day, as we were having a break from work, he drew a circle in the dust and asked us; 'Where you from?'

The first lad said 'Scotlando' and made a vague mark in the dirt.

The next lad said 'Waleso' and again made a mark in the dirt.

The next lad was Dutch so he said 'Hollando' and made a mark roughly where he thought Holland was on this quaint map of the world.

So he then asked Mick. As Mick was always proud of being Irish, he said 'Irelando' and again made a mark.

The guard said, 'Ah Hollando also'. 'No,' Mick said; 'f**king Irelando.'

'Ah Hollando also,' said the guard, not understanding the slight difference in pronunciation. Mick was getting angry and swore at the guard who chased him brandishing his rifle. We all shouted, 'Mick, tell him you're a flying Dutchman.'

A few days later we heard that the camp blacksmith needed two volunteers to help him make rivets for the railway. The British soldier was always taught never to volunteer for anything, but Mick and I volunteered mainly because we thought we might be able to scrounge some extra rice if we worked well for the blacksmith. The workshop was in a tent about a half mile from the camp and we were set to work with a seven pound hammer. Our job was to tap the end of white-hot bolts to make rivets whilst the blacksmiths held the bolts in a set of long tongs. One day I hit the chisel too hard and the end of the white-hot bolt shot off and struck me on the ankle. It penetrated to a depth of about two inches. The pain was excruciating and blood started to flow freely over the floor. The Japanese blacksmith got angry and knocked me to the ground with a blow to the head shouting the Japanese word, 'Kurrah.' Leaning on Mick's shoulder I was able to hobble back to the camp hospital hut, where the wonderful Doctor Roy cleaned and bandaged the wound.

That night the pain in my ankle prevented me from getting to sleep, but as I was totally exhausted I eventually drifted off into a troubled sleep only to be awoken in a sweat by a terrible nightmare. The devil appeared with his horns and pitchfork and began to smash all the holy relics off the altar. Then an angel appeared all in gold with a sword and shield and proceeded to knock the devil off the altar and replace the relics. Once again my mind started to play tricks on me during my dreams. To make matters worse, dysentery struck me for the first time whilst I was recovering from my ankle wound and I had to hop to the latrine pits and squat on the bamboo slats on one leg. I was terrified that I might fall into the mass of excreta and writhing insects below. Not for the first time since the war started, I really thought I was about to die. I was also suffering from further bouts of malaria as well as the dysentery and pain from my ankle, but Mick looked after me like a mother. He would go round the huts swapping cigarettes for the rice from dying men, as I said earlier a practice that we did on a regular basis. After a distressing week or so, (at least I think it was about a week), I began to feel better. Doctor Roy cleaned my wound regularly with saline solution. Mick told me later that the doctor had been concerned that I was going to lose my foot as gangrene nearly set in.

A few weeks later we were marched the seventeen miles or so to another camp called Thakhanun. The monsoon season was now well under way and the water poured down from the high ground above the camp, flooding our tents. It brought with it all the dead cats, rats and rotting garbage thrown into the river upstream by the natives. This made the camp a fertile environment for the propagation of the disease we all feared – 'Cholera'. The guards were terrified of catching this fatal disease and left us alone, staying at least half a mile away. They wore masks on their faces and left us to bury our own dead comrades. We had no medicines and the only thing that Dr Roy had to treat the disease was his 'saline solution'. He constantly stressed the importance of good hygiene: 'Before you eat, you must dip your spoons into the saline solution, and don't forget – your lives depend on it.' I saw one medical orderly wipe a cholera victim down, forget to wash his hands and smoke a cigarette – he was dead within forty-eight hours.

Cholera spread through the camp like wildfire. Someone in the bed next to you would be alive when you went out on a '*Speedo*' work detail in the morning and by the end of the shift, his bed space would be empty. At this camp my comrades were dying at the rate of ten a day and the Japanese instructed us to dig really deep pits to bury the bodies. One morning Doctor Roy asked for four volunteers to bury some bodies, so Mick and I, and two others, put up our hands. We walked about half a mile to a deep pit where five bodies lay wrapped in rice sacks with ropes tied round their ankles, stomachs and necks. We hurriedly lowered the first four bodies on ropes into the pit and as we began to lower the last one in, the sacking came off his face. I instantly recognised him as a young sergeant from the Norfolks. His face was wizened, wrinkled and yellow and his teeth had gone the same colour. It was a very sad moment for me as I remembered him from earlier days on the railway doing an impression of Harry Chapman (an old music hall star). Behind the guards' backs he would sing: 'Any old iron, any old iron.' Then do a little shuffle and sing, 'Boiled beef and carrots.' As I lowered him into the stinking pit a tear fell from my eye. A bit later the Japanese decided that it was better to burn the bodies rather than bury them and I was relieved not to be detailed any more to that horrible task. We could clearly see the flames and smoke from the fires at night, and smell the burning flesh.

Soon we marched on again a further forty-seven miles up country to a camp called Sonkurai. As we had come from a cholera camp we had to submit to the indignity of having a glass rod shoved up the anus or 'glass rodded' as we called it. This was to test if we were clear of the disease, but we never got to find out the results and of course we were just happy to be alive. Due to inadequate food, a lack of uncontaminated water and overwork we had little resistance to the threat of this dreaded disease, or the many others doing their rounds at the camps. Sonkurai was to be our last camp on this terrible railway project. We had marched a total of 190 miles from where we had started at Ban Pong. It was a minor miracle that both Mick and I had managed to make it this far.

Sonkurai was a much better camp than the others we had stayed in. Of course better is a relative word, as it was not difficult to improve on the primitive and inhumane conditions of the past camps. The Japanese gave us a water buffalo to share between 200 men, but I didn't find much of it in my rice ration. Mick asked the soldier in charge of killing the animal if we could have some of its blood and we took his grunt to mean yes. It looked like black pudding when mixed with our rice and kept us a bit better nourished for a few days.

As news of Allied victories began to filter through on the grapevine, many of us began to wonder if we would be able to face our colleagues after the war - assuming of course that we would win. Although we had done our best in the Malayan campaign, a feeling of letting the country down still permeated our thinking. Some of the lads even contemplated escape, but at Sonkurai the reality of the situation dispelled all such thoughts. Although we were not actually penned in by the usual wires and walls associated with prisons, we were more than incarcerated by the thick jungle and surrounding hills. To try to escape was a sure recipe for death in this alien environment so Mick and I settled down to make the best of the hand we had been dealt.

We were tortured not only physically but mentally by our captors, and also by the environment; torrential monsoon rains battered us ceaselessly and a variety of ills caused many of my comrades to depart this bleak world we were living in. But of course it was essential for survival not to admit defeat, as such admittance meant certain death. I was lucky to be with my mate Mick, as the word defeat was simply not in his Irish vocabulary.

It was now September 1943 and the railway was nearing completion some six months ahead of schedule, mainly due to the many 'Speedos' inflicted on us. The Japanese had started using it to transport their troops to the Burma front, where they had already taken the capital Rangoon, but the pressure on them by the Allies was increasing and they urgently needed to transport more troops and supplies to the front line. Still, the 'speedo' eased off and work on the railway was now only maintenance. By October it was virtually finished, except for some tidying up, and the Japanese began to give us more rest days. The extra days off work enabled us to make the camp more habitable, a great bonus to us after the rigours of the past few months. Conditions almost became 'luxurious' compared to previous conditions, even though we still had to exist on minimal rations. They even gave us Christmas Day 1943 off, in celebration of the completions of the railway, and to add to our 'holiday' some extra rice, whitebait fish and corned beef were provided. Our cooks made rice fishcakes and corned beef rissoles – delicious fare for men near to starvation. For one whole day I wasn't hungry any more and felt really good for the first time in many months. To top it off, they arranged a church service to pay tribute to those men who had died during the building of the railway.

I would be twenty-four in a few weeks and I began to think about home. Although my stomach was full, I despaired about ever seeing

England or my parents again and began to get very depressed. I had been in constant action for the ten weeks of the Malaya campaign, followed by nine months working on this bloody railway and my spirits were at an all time low. It was probably a blessing that I was unaware of the further hardships that were ahead of me over the next twenty months. Of course I could always depend on Mick to give me a lift when I felt down and as usual he started telling me his awful jokes.

That Christmas night in 1943 was very cold by Siamese standards with a full moon and in the camp we had a good old singsong. Mick sang his favourite 'The Mountains of Mourne', Bill Riley sang Irving Berlin's 'Always' and Ossie Osbourne sang a popular song of the 1930s called 'Home' which really brought tears to our eyes.

For the duration of our labours on the railway we had been sabotaging the project at every opportunity, mainly by burying rotten tree stumps covered in red ants into the embankments. On one occasion this caused a train carrying Japanese troops to de-rail. The soldiers had to jump off and unload their weapons and equipment before we were ordered to lift the train back onto the rails using a series of pulleys, wire ropes and long iron bars. It took a superhuman effort to get this huge train back on the rails but somehow we managed it, despite the beatings from the guards. We derived a great deal of satisfaction in getting one over on the enemy. They would humiliate us in front of their own troops saying that 'one hundred POWs - *samma, samma*, one elephant'.

We were unused to the hardships and diseases of the jungle and most of the lads died of exhaustion, starvation, beriberi, malaria or dysentery. Many boys actually died after the railway was completed as did others on their way back south towards Singapore. A tragic end to many young lives.

Chapter 8

The Hellships *Asaka Maru* and *Hakusan Maru*

With work on the railway finished we were told to pack up our belongings and be ready to move out of Sonkurai. It was around about the middle of February 1944 when we were finally lined up and marched down to the track and herded onto a train. The train was made up of the same kind of steel cattle trucks we had travelled up from Singapore in over a year earlier, and it took an eternity to travel the fifteen miles or so to the base camp at Thakhanun. The heat was unbearable as we crawled along at a snail's pace, stopping every few miles in sidings to allow trains packed with Japanese troops to pass on their journey north.

We spent a couple of weeks at Thakhanun camp before setting off again in a train to travel the 200 miles to the main base of Non Pladuk, a journey that had taken us two weeks on foot, but now took less than a day. It was a perilous trip and we were always afraid that some of the badly constructed embankments and bridges would collapse and all our efforts to stay alive would be ended below this 'awful' railway.

It was now spring 1944 and with the tide turning against them, the Japanese Navy was coming under intense pressure from the Americans in the Western Pacific and the South China Sea. Over the previous two years, they had stretched themselves to the limit on several fronts, and needed a sustained industrial effort back in the homelands to provide the necessary war materials to keep up their offensive and defend territories they had conquered. With most of their able-bodied men away fighting the war, they were short of labourers to keep their industries going to support the war effort. But of course the Japanese had already proved that they were ruthless towards their captives and found a ready solution to this problem. They simply shipped the POWs back to Japan to make up the shortfall. This happened throughout the Far East as fit men were transported to Japan; if you could stand up you were classed as fit. Initially they asked for skilled men and at Non Pladuk we were lined up in front of the officer in charge. It was an amusing sight. He sat behind a large table in the middle of a clearing with his sword in front of him and a pet monkey on his shoulder. He then asked each one of us if we had a trade in England. The first bloke was a carpenter and he was immediately pushed to one side. 'You Japan,' grunted the officer. Word quickly spread down the line that if you did not admit to having a trade then you just might get out of being sent to Japan. At that point everyone started telling the officer that they were a window cleaner. When it came to Mick's turn he said, 'Me window cleaner – me clean Crystal Palace.' Of course we all burst out into fits of laughter but the officer began to get very agitated and shouted. 'All Blitish solders pukking winda cleaners.' In the end it didn't matter anyway because if you were able to stand you were chosen and we were told, 'Now you go to the land of the cherry blossom.'

'Maybe we'll be working in a shoe polish factory,' I jokingly whispered to Mick.

Many of the very ill POWs were also chosen to go and when Dr Roy protested about their condition and ability to withstand the voyage, he was savagely beaten to the ground. By this time however we had resigned ourselves to the fact that it didn't really matter anymore and at least we would still be together.

The Japanese only chose white POWs to be taken to Japan. They were concerned about the possibility of mixing their race, bit strange really as there was little likelihood of a POW getting to sleep with a Japanese woman. Even if he did there was little chance of any of them being able to 'perform' as it were, with the state of our health. They were also concerned that gays should not be taken; how they would know was anybody's guess, as sex with either men or women was the last thing on our minds.

At Non Pladuk we were told that we would soon be setting off for Bangkok where we would board a ship to Japan, but after spending several weeks at the camp we began to wonder if this was indeed true. The days dragged by and weeks turned into months before, on 11 June, we were eventually loaded onto the same decrepit railway trucks for the journey back to Singapore. Once again fortune was on my side and that guardian angel was still looking after me, as some three months later the Non Pladuk camp was almost flattened by Allied bombers. Their target was the nearby railway sidings and several stray bombs hit the camp killing around eighty British and Dutch POWs.

The four-day journey south was almost as bad as the previous one some fifteen months earlier. Again it was a nightmare with little food and drink, but fortunately we were able to scrounge bananas off the locals when the train made some of its regular stops. We pulled into Singapore station as dawn was breaking on 16 June. By now, Mick and I were once again completely exhausted and at the end of our physical and mental endurance. The very thought of food drove us insane and we would have happily killed the first person we saw with food in their hands. The only consolation was that we were on our way back to Changi and I was sure that the boys would have a sumptuous feast ready for us when we got there. We were then unceremoniously shoved onto lorries and driven down to Changi, where the sumptuous feast failed to materialise as food was desperately short down on the island as well. Here at least, we had a meal of sorts and a good sleep for the night.

The next day we were ordered to form up ready to be addressed by the senior Japanese officer, Colonel Nakamura. We were soon to be transported to Japan and he wanted to tell us all about the delights in store for us. I managed to obtain a copy of his speech from my good friend Harold Skinner's Booklet:

'You are to be transferred from the jurisdiction of POW camp, Thailand, to that of Japan where you are to resume labour duties. Since the opening of the Thailand POW camps you were diligently carrying out imposed labour duty for more than twenty months. Especially you were employed in railway construction in which your discharge of duty attained aimed objective as scheduled, for which we appreciate warmly.

On completion of above mentioned, you will be transferred to the Holy Land of the Rising Sun, where scenery is simply superb.

The Emperor of Great Japan, proper appellation Bis-Y-Yasima Dai Nippon Takoken, is populaced with nationals of up-righteousness, acts of morality, brave yet courteous, humanious, but strictly severe on vices. The proverb most common in use thereof: "Even hunter himself will not slay a strayed bird seek refuge on her lap" will properly explain the attitude of Japanese sentiments.

The land has four distinct seasons; Spring – with abundance of various blossoms, where birds chirp peaceful everywhere; evergreen Summer – with cool breezes easing the universe; transparent Autumn sky with clement moon; and with Winter, in which snow whitewashes the whole country, purifying the inhabitants.

These are nothing but the image and reflection of His august Majesty's greater virtues, to which all nationals are bound to follow in loyalty towards the Imperial family and filial piety towards parents, creation of benevolency, etc., etc. to eternal efforts.

Therefore, I tell you, officers and men, go to Japan with ease of mind and do your imposed duty to perfection. Then I verily tell you that our billion nationals will be welcoming you to share the imperial favour with you.

On the other hand, should any one of you still retain conscience of any eniminal nationals, and project or proceed things up against to the interest of Japan, consequential results must be borne on his own shoulders, however regrettable to all concerned.

I re-iterate, believe in Japanese chivalry and go forward in the right way not astraying on proper and mature consideration.

In conclusion, I should like to call your attention to take good care of your health for the sudden change in climatical conditions and wish you the happy future.

With my blessing for your "Bon Voyage".

Col. Nakamura.'

'Sounds a nice place but anything must be better than that dammed railway,' I said to Mick.

'Let's just wait and see Johnny,' he replied.

We were blissfully unaware at the time that a previous convoy of some nineteen ships, along with five escorts, had been attacked by American submarines in the East China Sea. One of the escorts was torpedoed and sunk. It was probably a blessing in disguise that we were not aware of the great dangers we were to face over the coming weeks.

The Japanese issued us with a pair of boots, shirt and a colourful pair of shorts for the voyage, probably because they did not want their population to see thousands of walking skeletons in G-strings arriving in their country. We were named Japan Party Number 2 and as soon the colonel had finished his speech, we were herded onto lorries and driven the few miles down to Singapore docks. 750 of us were then unceremoniously dumped onto the baking hot concrete with our meagre belongings. We were ordered by the guards to sit down in rows on the quayside alongside a ship nestling against the side of the dock for what seemed like hours, but what was in reality about three.

'How the hell are we all going to get on board that?' I whispered to Mick.

'It will be a bit cosy, Johnny,' said Mick in his usual jovial way. But of course neither of us realised at the time that that this rusting hulk would become more than 'cosy' over the coming weeks.

The ship we were about to board was the 4,600 ton *Asaka Maru* (*Maru* being the Japanese for ship). Ironically the *Asaka Maru* was originally a British ship. She had been built at John Brown's shipyard on the Clyde in 1894 and was originally called the *Glasgow Belle*, but this vessel looked like no 'belle' in the literal sense of the word. It had been sold by Britain to the Japanese in 1934 at a bargain price and had sailed from Japan a year previously, bringing troops to Singapore. She had then sailed to Java to pick up Indonesian and Dutch POWs bound for New Guinea and then returned to Singapore to pick up her 'human' cargo. The *Asaka* looked to us like a 4,600 ton death trap (which is exactly what it turned out to be).

We were then lined up in front of a big pile of rubber blocks shaped like petrol cans. We were each ordered to pick one up and marched up onto the deck. These blocks were supposed to be our life jackets! My block was quite heavy and I was convinced that it would sink rather than float if we ever had the misfortune to use it. My misgivings were confirmed when one of the lads dropped a block into the harbour where it sank like a stone to the bottom. I said a quick prayer as I picked mine up and followed the lads up the gangplank. The Japanese were of course up to their usual cunning tricks. These 'lifejackets' were their way of transporting over 750 blocks of rubber back to Japan, as we were ordered to hand them in when we arrived (if indeed we ever did arrive).

I was horrified when the guards pushed us down a ladder into a stinking black hold and indeed my premonitions about what was to follow became very real. As I looked up towards the hatch all I could see were bodies falling down on top of us, legs and feet everywhere; the feeling of claustrophobia was frightening. The hold was low, not much higher than twelve feet and had a wooden rack running right round. We were crammed in so tight that that it was impossible to lie down so we had to squat on our haunches and any attempt to move around was an ordeal. The lack of air in the hold quickly became unbearable and I really felt that I was encased in a steel tomb.

'I don't think we can last more than a few hours in here,' I whispered to Mick in a state of panic.

'Stick with it Johnny, and we'll be OK,' he responded in his usual positive way.

As I settled down in the stinking evil hold, the full reality of the situation hit me for the first time, especially when they battened down the hatches. Two out of every three of us were still suffering from dysentery, malaria, beriberi or jungle ulcers and there were emaciated bodies everywhere, lying around like rag dolls in a dark steel box. Rats were running across our faces and I felt doomed. Some of the boys began to panic. The heat was unbearable and many were screaming to be let out, but I knew that if we tried to rush the hatches we would be killed by the Japanese. We had no choice but to try and make ourselves as comfortable as possible in the wretched conditions. We were so hungry that we would have eaten anything and I quickly demolished the meagre portion of rice, gravy powder and powdered whitebait covered in weevils given to us. We lay naked on the wooden shelves fixed to the side of the hold. It was exhausting even to move but we managed to fix lines across the hold to which we attached our G-strings or any other bits of clothing we could find. We took it in turns to swing the strings from side to side just to get some sort of air movement. We hardly spoke as it was so much of an effort just to breathe in the foul conditions.

The crew of the *Asaka Maru* was made up of a motley bunch of Japanese teenagers and old salts reaching the end of their maritime career, along with a few soldiers and six cooks. They certainly did not fill us with confidence that we would reach Japan in one piece. When all the POWs were on board, we cast off and moved slowly out of Singapore harbour. We were now the responsibility of Captain Odake Bunji and his crew and it was his job to get us safely to Japan; Lieutenant Ino Takeo was in charge of us POWs. As soon as we had pulled away from the harbour wall, Captain Bunji issued orders for some of us to be allowed on deck, on the understanding that we would not cause any trouble and that we would get ourselves organised. Quite frankly I think he was concerned that he would end up delivering a boat load of corpses if he kept us all below. It was a huge relief when I climbed out, even though it was blazing hot on the deck as the sun bounced off the metal decking. A hosepipe had been rigged up and we were able to have a 'shower' once a day, but of course it was sea water and you still did not feel clean. Our officers were then issued with a set of boat orders for the trip, which they read out to us to much laughter; especially regulations 3 and 6 (see Appendix 1).

As we edged out of the harbour I noticed a German submarine tied up at one of the jetties. The crew were moving about with great efficiency on the deck in their clean white naval uniforms and I felt a tinge of envy for our European neighbours, even though I was well aware we were at war against them back home. It made me feel even more inhuman and embarrassed that they should see me in a state of filth and squalor, so I quickly looked away. For some reason, I did not share the same hatred for the Germans as I did for the Japanese.

Soon we rounded Blakan Mati island and then, oddly, came to a halt near to St. John's Island. Apparently the Japanese were going to form a convoy so we had to wait for other ships to join us. We expected to sit at anchor for maybe a few hours before moving on, but the hours dragged into days and the days dragged into weeks – in the end we sat at anchor in this hell-hole for sixteen days. Fortunately we were allowed to stay on deck for most of the time as conditions in the hold were unbearable. Even though there was no shade on the deck, the tropical heat was preferable to conditions in the hold. We got some relief at night when the temperature dropped, but space was very limited with the large number of men squashed together on deck. Meanwhile, the Japanese crew took it in turns to go ashore whilst we waited and our interpreter managed to get one of them to bring back a copy of the Singapore paper, the *Syonan Times*. This paper was surreptitiously passed around and we were all heartened to discover that D-Day had taken place and even more importantly for us, the Americans had invaded the Mariannas Islands.

Our convoy was called SHIMI-5 and consisted of ten ships accompanied by the torpedo boat *Sagi* and two minesweepers. As well as the *Asaki*, the group was made up of the *Olympia Maru*, *Kurogano Maru*, *Mexico Maru*, *Shirahato Maru*, and the No 6 *Kyoei Maru*. The other ships containg POWs were the *Rashin Maru* (containing 1065 POWs), *Sekito Maru* (1024 POWs), *Hofuku Maru* (1287 POWs) and the *Hakushita Maru* (609 POWs). We were to be the largest group of POWs shipped to Japan during the entire war.

It was 4 July 1944, ironically American Independence Day, when this whole comical convoy of ten wrecks, loaded with over 5,000 Allied prisoners of war, set off for the land of the rising sun. As Singapore fell away behind us, we passed the tropical islands of Pulaw Batau and Palau Bintan before leaving the last point of Malaya, Tanjong Penyosoh and heading on towards Labuan. By this time conditions on board were inhumane and every one of us was in a state of great physical and mental distress. The latrine was a large wooden box lashed to the side of the ship with an opening in the middle and a ledge on either side for your feet. With dysentery still rife there was always a constant queue to use this primitive contraption, with some men going up to fifteen times a day. Matters were made even worse as the inside of the box was slippery from the blood excreted by the dysentery sufferers. My bare feet would often slip as I squatted down and I was terrified of being washed into the sea when a big wave broke or the ship rolled. You really had to hang on with all your strength; I saw one man tragically get washed away as he was so weak that he was unable to hang on. When we reported this to the Japanese guards they just shrugged their shoulders and turned away, completely oblivious to our distress and suffering. To them another POW's death was probably one less living prisoner to deal with. We had no toilet paper and had to use what we could find or scrounge, including pages from the few books left in our possession.

Malaria also broke out again with a vengeance onboard and as we had almost no quinine, we all had to suffer the dreadful effects of this awful disease. Beriberi was also on the increase. Many of my comrades were to die on this fateful voyage and we wrapped them in rice sacks and tipped them into the sea. Not even a prayer was said as they were consigned to a grave somewhere in the depths of the ocean.

After two days sailing, we reached the coast of Borneo, the third largest island in the world, and dropped anchor near North Borneo. Whilst on deck I could see in the distance Kinabalu Mountain, the highest peak in the Crocker Range at over 6,000 feet. The next morning we sailed on again up the coast of Palawan, a wild and rugged island, part of the Philippines group, before entering the port of Miri on 8 July. We stayed at anchor in Miri for two days before the convoy was reorganised and named convoy MI-08. The *Hofuka Maru* and the *Shirahato Maru* stayed at Miri whilst eight other ships joined us, increasing the convoy to nineteen ships. Two new escorts also joined us, the CDV *Mikura* and the torpedo boat *Hiyondori*.

On 10 July we moved on again up the coast. Six days later we passed between the tip of the Bataan peninsula and Corregidor island eventually entering Manila Bay in the Philippines, where we dropped anchor. I prayed that we would be put ashore and allowed off this disgusting ship for the first time in a month, but it was not to be. The Japanese were anxious that we should continue on our journey to the 'land of the rising sun.'

For the next three weeks we sat either in the oppressive heat of the hold, or on the deck covered in coal dust and soaked by the torrential downpours whilst the new convoy was made ready to sail. The loading of coal was done by Filipino labourers and again we were able to obtain a copy of the local paper from the sympathetic Filipinos, many of whom spoke good English. The paper confirmed that the Americans had taken the Mariannas and that an invasion of the Philippines was expected any day. It brought us news of the Normandy campaign and again we were buoyed by the news of Allied successes. All this was of course tempered by our own predicament and the thought was never far from my mind that my life could come to a swift and terrible end at any time.

On 8 August, as part of convoy MATA-26, we eventually set off out of Manilla towards the northern tip of Luzon and Formosa. In some respects we were fortunate to have remained in Manila, as on the same day we left, two of our original convoy were sunk by the American submarine USS *Barbel* in the East China Sea.

We passed Corregidor just after dark. To avoid detection, all the ships had their lights out or covered up and it was a pitch-black night. By dawn we neared the coast and it appeared that the convoy had got split up during the night as there were only two or three other ships in the vicinity and our escorts seemed to have vanished. We entered Lyngayen Bay on the tenth, where again we waited for a couple of days before setting off towards the northern end of Luzon and out into the China Sea.

The next day the crew began to get particularly jumpy. This may have been caused by the sight of dead Japanese soldiers floating past, their bodies horrendously bloated and kept afloat by their life jackets, or from the news of other ships being sunk. We were well aware that American submarines were operating in the area and that the risk of being sunk by a torpedo was great.

'We better stick together and get ready to abandon ship if we get hit,' I said to Mick.

The crew began to get even more agitated and some of them started to prepare rice balls. They donned two suits of clothes and hats and sat on life-rafts with all their personal possessions. Not a very reassuring sight but quite an amusing one. Apparently they were preparing themselves for the 'afterlife' where they would need the extra suits of clothing. We discovered that one of the other ships in the convoy had been sunk by an American submarine and that our guards were terrified as they were sure we would be next. One of the soldiers began to swivel round the old army field gun that had been bolted to the deck. How they were to fight off a submarine with that rusting hulk of a gun was anyone's guess. By now at least two more ships in our convoy were sunk and it was rumoured that one of them contained a group of Japanese nurses on their way home, but of course rumours were always rife on board and we had no way of confirming this.

On 13 August we were about one hundred miles out from Luzon when a terrific gale blew up and the ship began to roll and toss violently. We clung on to anything we could find as huge waves broke over the starboard side of the ship. Many of the men who were on deck began to run for the sanctuary of the stinking hold, but there was just no way I was going down there again. Several of the POWs who had gone a bit mad had been put down below and I certainly didn't want to be in their company. I was determined to stay on deck and take my chance in the storm.

I looked around for Mick but he had vanished. I just prayed that he hadn't been washed overboard as to lose my best mate after what we had been through would have been devastating. I felt very alone and afraid.

Hanging on tightly I made my way slowly up some iron steps to an upper deck where I was able to find some shelter behind a bulkhead. Although I was frightened, for some reason a strange feeling of elation came over me. All the crew had disappeared and it was the first time in two and a half years that I felt free from them. Most of them had locked themselves in their cabins. I was well aware that I was still a prisoner, many miles from home but this temporary respite from their bullying and beatings gave me a real lift, despite the fact that the ship was in grave danger. As I clung onto the metal stairway, huge waves swept over the ship washing away anything that was not securely fixed down. Large iron boilers and ice chests were ripped away from their fixings and water crashed and flowed all over the decks. Gazing out over the wind-lashed sea I could just make out in the distance an oil tanker blazing furiously and I could see that this was slowly disappearing from view. We began to take in water through a damaged hatch and the hull was starting to crack in several places flooding the holds. Anyone still down below was wallowing in several inches of sea water. The *Asaka* had been damaged several months earlier when it had been hit by a torpedo and the poorly repaired welds were beginning to open again.

The storm raged throughout the night and as dawn broke things were starting to get desperate as the pumps could not keep up with the ingress of water. With the daylight we were able to see what a difficult position we were in. The ship was in a small bay near a rocky shoreline about a couple of hundred yards away and was listing heavily to starboard with huge waves still breaking over us. All the pumps had packed in and it was a miracle that we were still afloat. The latrine box was washed overboard and the decks were running with vomit and excreta. Suddenly I heard a familiar voice.

'Where the f**king hell have you been, Johnny?'

I was relieved to hear the sound of Mick's Irish brogue again. He had made a dash for the hold whilst I stayed on deck.

By now we were both starving and, as we hadn't eaten for three days, we decided to break into the crew's quarters to look for food. The ship was in such a bad state that all the crew were manning the lifeboats ready to abandon ship, so we reckoned that their quarters would be empty. In one room we found some burnt rice casings in a sack – probably being taken to Japan to feed cattle, but we were so hungry that we gorged ourselves on these burnt offerings. Down in the holds the conditions were terrible. Many of the lads, who had been ill when the storm broke, were by now in an even worse state despite the superhuman efforts of our medical orderlies. The smell coming up from down below was overpowering and I was determined that I was not going to go back down there, even if it meant being swept overboard. When the crew realised that the ship was not going to sink immediately, they returned to their quarters to find that the POWs had looted most of their personal belongings as well as most of their food. They were furious but there was little they could do as survival was the only thing on their minds.

It was now around 15 August and as the day wore on the ship began to list more and more to starboard, making it difficult to stand up without hanging onto something. Although the storm had blown itself out, the sea was still rough. Waves were still buffeting us and the water levels in the holds began to rise. We were given buckets and formed a human chain from the holds to try and bale out in a futile effort to stem the rising water. I knew the game was up when the rats started running across the deck and jumping over the side. I guess they knew before us that the ship was doomed.

As dusk fell we heard an almighty bang followed by a great crunching noise. The ship had struck rocks and began to list even more heavily to starboard. The ship's siren and bells rang out constantly and I was convinced that the end was nigh.

'This is it Johnny, stay close we're sinking. Grab your rubber block,' Mick said.

I sat terrified, clutching my rubber block alongside Mick. We heard the hiss of the steam as the valves were opened and then suddenly all was quiet, peaceful even, as the ship settled on the rocks.

For the rest of the night we sat clutching our rubber blocks not daring to make a move as we waited for the crew to tell us to abandon ship. The only noise we could hear was the waves breaking on the nearby rocks and I fully expected the ship to break in two at any moment.

When dawn broke we were able to see that we had struck rocks and the ship was firmly settled on them. We were in a small bay about 300 yards from the shore and someone said that the Captain had deliberately run the ship aground rather than risk us sinking out to sea. Waves were still crashing over us but after a time everything became quiet and calm. In the distance we could see the coast. It was so close that we could see people working in the fields; they would stop work now and then to gaze out over the choppy water at the stricken ship, as though it was some sort of movie and they were waiting for the final thrilling instalment to take place.

'I hope we don't have to swim ashore,' I said to Mick.

'If we do I'll help you Johnny,' he replied.

Of course I knew that Mick was a strong swimmer but neither of us was in any fit state to attempt to swim the 300 yards through those heavy seas.

Other than the burnt rice casings we had not eaten anything for two days and were, as usual, absolutely starving. There was no chance of any cooking as all the rice had gone anyway. The only food that was available to us was the same hard burnt remnants of the rice that had been scraped off the bottom of pans after each meal. The Japanese had been saving these 'burnt offerings' for use as pig feed back in Japan and they had been stored in bags down below. They now dragged these bags up on deck and we were issued with a pitifully small portion along with a piece of fish and some seaweed. It tasted horrible but at least it was something to ease the hunger pangs.

For two days we sat on the stricken ship, firmly wedged on the rocks, waiting for help that never seemed to come. Several of the lads who had been really ill passed away as we waited, their bodies tipped over the side into the shallow waters of the bay. We were now without any food or water and the situation was becoming really desperate, but for some reason we felt elated. We had convinced ourselves that we would be picked up by the Americans, but this hope was short lived as, on the sixteenth, two Japanese destroyers approached and tried to get lines over to us. As the sea was still very rough this proved to be an impossible task so our crew began to try and launch one of our lifeboats. They were obviously not very experienced in this task as one of the ropes broke sending the lifeboat crashing down into the sea; it promptly drifted away towards the beach. The crew then managed to launch a second lifeboat successfully and some of the lads were ordered to jump down into it. It was bouncing off the side of the ship and how no one was injured I do not know as it was about a fifteen-foot drop. The lifeboat eventually got away from the side of the ship and, half-full of men, headed for one of the destroyers. This operation took over an hour so the crew of the destroyers decided to launch their own lifeboats and start a shuttle service from the doomed vessel. Mick and I managed to squeeze into one of the tightly packed boats and a few minutes later we pulled alongside one of the destroyers. It was nearly dark by now and with great difficulty we climbed up the rope ladder they had hung over the side. I smacked my ankle as I climbed up and was very nearly sick, but Mick, who had climbed up ahead of me, pulled me up the last few yards onto the deck.

When all the POWs and crew of the *Asaka Maru* were on board, the destroyer set off and sailed through the night at high speed. It was a relief to settle back on the warm deck, even though there were hundreds of us with barely room to move. We hadn't eaten since the burnt rice three days earlier and we were both absolutely famished. Not for the first time I had a bit of good luck. Right next to me was a large metal container, about the size of an oil drum. It was open on one side and as I slid my hand in I was amazed to find lots of hard little square things. I pulled one out and discovered it was a biscuit. I tasted it and passed it to Mick. By chance we were lying beside a box containing the crew's supply of hardtack biscuits. It was dark so I was able to slide my hand in again and again to steal a few biscuits. My heart was beating wildly and I was terrified I would get caught and get a good beating. I shoved a few biscuits into Mick's hand. 'God bless you, Johnny,' he said. I must have pinched at least ten biscuits before deciding that the risk of getting caught was too great. We slowly chewed on the biscuits, trying to be as quiet as possible and for the first time in weeks I felt calm and peaceful. It's strange what a few biscuits can mean to a starving man.

The crew of the Japanese destroyer treated us well and I am sure some of them even felt sorry for us. The sailors seemed a cut above their army counterparts as they were all smartly dressed and very disciplined. They really looked after many of the lads who were ill and gave us food and cigarettes. By dawn we were steaming through the Pescadores Islands and early afternoon saw us near to Formosa. We were so close to the coast that I could clearly see the towns and villages on the island and even a train running along the shoreline. Just before nightfall we docked at a place called Keelung on North Formosa. We had no idea what they were going to do with us, but I felt fairly sure that we would be put us ashore as the destroyer had other more pressing duties to attend to.

'Maybe they will keep us in Formosa instead of Japan', I said to Mick.

'Doubt it, Johnny,' he replied. 'They'll find some way of getting us to the land of the f**king rising sun.'

The crew of the Japanese destroyer ferried us in launches onto the quayside and supplied us with food in containers for which we very thankful, a decent gesture that left us with a great deal of respect for the Japanese navy. By now we were down to just over 700 men as around fifty had died aboard the *Asaka Maru*.

We sat on the quayside for a few hours before being herded onto a barge, normally used to transport coal, and ferried out to another large ship sitting anchor in the bay. This ship was twice as big as the *Asaka Maru* and looked like a modern passenger liner. As we approached I could see the name of our new cruise liner clearly on the hull – the *Hakusan Maru*. It certainly looked a great deal better than the *Asaka* and our hopes soared at the thought of some decent accommodation for the final part of our journey to Japan.

The ship we were about to board for the final leg was built in Japan in 1923 as an all first-class passenger liner, capable of carrying 175 passengers and 200 crew. It was around 10,000 tons, over 500 feet long and could cruise at up to 16 knots. Prior to the war the *Hakusan* worked the lucrative Yokohama to Hamburg route and when war broke out it was commandeered by the Japanese Navy as a troop ship. As we approached I could see that she was carrying quite a few civilian passengers, many of them women and children who were staring down at us with intense interest. The captain of the *Hakusan Maru* was not at all happy that he had been landed with more than 700 POWs, many of whom were very ill and malnourished. Once again we were unceremoniously bundled down into a hold which realistically could only accommodate about half of our number and a feeling of dread came over me again as I stumbled down the ladder. The Japanese insisted that that the dysentery cases should be left on the top deck, along with most of the rest of the men who were suffering from a variety of ailments, where they were looked after by another wonderful doctor – Doctor Leadbetter. The doctor did his best to make our ill men as comfortable as possible. As well as the

Japanese civilians, the *Hakusan Maru* had picked up survivors from other shipwrecked vessels, along with soldiers from the Japanese 60 Regiment on their way back to Japan.

The hold of our new ship was even worse than that of the *Asaka Maru*. Although it was quite clean, there was no air, it was overcrowded and the heat was unbearable. We lay naked on wooden shelves, sweating profusely, and it was an effort to even move. To try and get some sort of air movement, again we resorted to stringing our G-strings and bits of clothing on a line across the hold and took it in turn to swing it back and forwards. We were in almost complete darkness, except for one small low-powered bulb swaying in the corridor which threw a small shaft of light over us. We sat in the gloom, sweating profusely, and waiting for the ship to weigh anchor on the final leg of our journey. That evening we were given our first meal, and it was reasonably good, considering how bad the food had been on the *Asaka*. Some delicious stew with pork and vegetables, but unfortunately there was not much of it, and I wolfed it down in a matter of seconds.

After a most uncomfortable night, we were let up onto the deck the next morning for some fresh air and the cool breeze was wonderful. However, I was well aware that we would soon be sent below again into that oven of a hold and I dreaded it. On the second day we were ordered up onto deck to be 'glass rodded' again to check if anyone had dysentery or cholera. This was done by a woman doctor, at least I assumed she was a doctor, who sat at a table on her own and never smiled or spoke as she shoved a glass rod up 300 or so arses. She must really have drawn the short straw to be given that awful task. There were skinny backsides, sore backsides and backsides with ringworm. The other passengers crowded the upper decks to observe this humiliating procedure and seemed to take a great deal of enjoyment out of seeing our naked rear ends. As your name was called out you had to go up to the table, bow, turn around, drop your trousers and take the rod. You then pulled your trousers back up, turned again, bowed and went back into line.

Eventually, on 22 August we weighed anchor and left Keelung heading for the port of Moji in Kyushu, the most southerly of the

Japanese islands – a distance of around one thousand miles. As the days dragged by, things in that oppressive hold got even worse. Every night at least two of the lads passed away from disease and/or starvation, and I was just about at breaking point on many occasions. Mick was again a tower of strength for me with his ready wit and never failing optimism. Things got a little better after a few days when the captain, after continual protests from our medical officers, opened one of the forward holds for some of our most sick men. This meant we were able to segregate the dysentery cases and slow down the rate of cross-infection, but at least two or three men died each night in that forward hold.

After six or seven days at sea, a rumour spread around that we were nearing Japan. I certainly hoped and prayed that I would soon get off that stinking vessel. During the last few nights we could hear the sound of explosions on both sides of the ship and when the alarm buzzer went off one evening I began to panic. The watertight doors were slammed shut each night and if we had been hit we would have had no chance of escape from that crowded hold. Somebody shouted, 'We've been hit, every man for himself.' Pandemonium erupted as men began to clamber over each other and fights broke out. We were all suffocating from the lack of air.

'We're trapped,' I said to Mick.

'Don't lose your nerve now, Johnny. Just keep quiet and wait,' he replied.

Mick always was the sort of man to be with in a crisis and he kept me calm in this potentially dangerous situation. After about an hour or so, the engines began to throb again and things became quiet once more, to everyone's immense relief.

On 28 August, almost eight weeks after leaving Singapore, we docked at a place called Moji on Kysushu Island where our clothes were removed and we had to take a disinfectant bath. We stood around naked in a huge warehouse, whilst waiting our turn for the 'bath'. At least we got our first 'reasonable' meal in weeks – a small box of rice with whitebait fish. The Japanese then issued us with 'new' clothes, or more accurately second-hand Dutch uniforms captured from the Dutch when they occupied Dutch Indo China.

'Perhaps things will get better for us, now we are in the land of the cherry blossom,' I said cynically to Mick.

The horrors of that trip from Singapore to Japan in those two hell ships will live in my mind until the day I die. Even today, I pray for the souls of those brave lads who survived the Malayan Campaign and horrors of the death railway, only to die in the dark, smelly, sweaty hold of a Japanese ship. During the fifty-six days of that voyage many men died. Many more arrived in a perilous state, hanging onto their lives by a thread. I have no idea, some sixty-four years later, how my colleagues were affected by those two sea journeys to Japan, but I can tell you that even today when I close my eyes I can still see that filthy, stinking hold, smell the stale odours of sick, shit, urine and death. I can still hear the cries for help from my fellow POWs.

Chapter 9

Japan

At Moji we were placed under the command of a group of smart looking Japanese soldiers. When they found out about the horrors of our voyage through their interpreter, they were most sympathetic and helpful; they provided us with better food and seemed really concerned for our sick men.

From Moji we made the short sea crossing to Shimoneseki on Honshu Island and then travelled on, by train, to Osaka – a distance of around 300 miles. The train journey took about twelve hours and again we were given reasonable food – usually a box of steamed rice with some fish and vegetables cooked in some sort of sauce. It tasted delicious, especially after the horrible fare we had been served on the ships. It was a great relief to sit on proper train seats and take in the vista of the Japanese countryside as we made our way towards the city. I was amazed that almost every inch of land was cultivated and crops of all kinds were growing – the Japanese certainly knew how to make the best use of their fertile land. As we neared Osaka, which the Japanese claimed was one of the largest cities in the Orient, the cultivated fields made way for vast industrial complexes. These reminded me of the factories in south London: such thoughts made me feel sad and homesick.

From Osaka we travelled on again, by train, for half an hour or so to the city of Amagasaki. It was now late August 1944 and the camp which was to be our home had high fencing all round and was heavily guarded around the perimeter with two armed guards manning the entrance. I couldn't quite understand why they were so paranoid about security because even if we did escape from the camp we would have been quickly recaptured and heavily punished.

Amagasaki camp was opened on 20 January 1943 and when we arrived, there were already some 200 British POWs in residence. They had been transferred from Hong Kong when it fell and had been there for over eighteen months. After just a few hours Mick and I realised that this was not going be a holiday camp. We were each given a number and another green uniform with a peaked hat; the uniforms had been taken from the Dutch when the Japanese invaded Java and were totally unsuitable for a Japanese winter, having been designed for wear in the tropics.

The camp commander was Warrant Officer Kozo Inagaki and the camp was made up of a series of wooden huts, each housing around 300 prisoners. There were two tiers of bunks and to get to the top tier you had to climb a ladder and fight for a bed space – there was just no room. We lay side by side, head to toe squashed like ants and surrounded by our bits of sacking and mess tins. There was no room to even turn over or stretch and there was always someone's stinking feet in your face. The smell of wet clothing drying on our bodies, urine from beriberi sufferers and faeces from the dysentery, made you retch.

'I think this is going to be hell when the weather gets bad,' I said to Mick.

'Don't worry, Johnny, we have survived up to now and we are not giving up,' he chirped.

After giving us just one day to settle in, we were marched to work in a factory that made metal fabrications for the Japanese Navy. It seems that the Japanese Army had sold on this ready made workforce of POWs and we were allocated to a man called Otani who specialised in marine contracts (and was reputedly a Japanese millionaire). The factory made lathes for the Japanese Navy and there must have been around two thousand civilians already working there. Otani was responsible for providing us with accommodation, uniforms, food and wages. The Army were still responsible for guarding us and ensuring that we got to and from work.

Conditions during the first couple of months at Amagasaki camp were not too bad as it was autumn and the weather was fine. Food was scarce though and Mick and I were constantly hungry, though we were not to know what problems the forthcoming winter was to bring.

It was about a fifteen minute walk to the factory from the camp and we had to be there for 0650 hrs each morning. On arrival we had to stand in line along with the civilian workers to be counted for *tenko*. It was compulsory to count in Japanese. Up to ten was quite easy '*iche, ne, san, si, go, rook, shichi, hachi, ku, ju*' but it got a bit more difficult above ten so everyone would rush to the front of the line because you would get a bashing if you could not remember the number. We then all had to salute the factory official in charge of the *tenko* and turn to the east to face the rising sun and clap our hands. You can imagine what the boys thought of this pointless exercise and things got even worse when we all had to do five minutes of exercises to the calls of '*ooshah, ooshah.*' I've no idea what it meant.

Our job was to load pig-iron into large trucks: when a truck was filled it was taken away by crane and tipped into barges moored along the canal which ran alongside the factory. A day's shift lasted eight hours and the only rest we got was for two or three minutes between loading. Even then the guards were on our backs, finding small jobs for us to do. The days dragged endlessly. We had been there for around a month when one evening the camp descended into chaos as we were eating our paltry meal of rice and stew. The guards came rushing into our hut shouting and screaming for us to follow them. Apparently there had been a warning of an extraordinary high tide and that the reclaimed land on which the camp and factories had been built was in great danger of flooding and they needed help to move all the food and stores onto platforms. We moved all the stores as quickly as possible and watched as the waters slowly rose in the camp from the safety of our upper bed platforms. It was a worrying sight as the water carried all sorts of rubbish and sewage, but fortunately the high tide didn't last long and the water slowly subsided to leave us with the problem of cleaning up the camp. We spent several days getting things back to normal and hoped that this was just a freak high tide and we would not be subjected to such a problem again.

It was now late November 1944 and winter was starting to set in.

The temperature was dropping dramatically, particularly during the night and with our meagre supply of blankets it was impossible to stay warm. Most nights I lay awake shivering violently and waiting for sunrise, it was almost a bonus to get up and walk to work but when we got there, things were not much better. Both ends of the factory were open and there was very little shelter from the incessant wind and rain. We were constantly cold, exacerbated by the lack of food and the fact that our bodies had become accustomed to the tropical temperatures of Thailand and Malaya. Although we didn't know it at the time Japan was about to experience her coldest ever winter since records began. I was thoroughly miserable and depressed and even Mick, who was normally cheerful, got very down at times. One day when the temperature dropped below zero he said to me, 'so this is the land of the f**king rising sun'. As Christmas approached, the temperatures began to drop even more and with the *benjo* (toilet) outside, men with dysentery had to trample over you to get to the ladder. Often they would not make it on time, leaving their shit everywhere.

One morning as we walked to work I noticed a louse biting the back of Mick's neck. I couldn't resist plucking it out and got a painful whack on the back of my hand from the guard for doing so: we were then all made to stand in the biting cold wind for fifteen minutes as a punishment. Again the cruelty of the Japanese guards made our life a complete misery. To add to our woes, colonies of bedbugs and lice multiplied rapidly in our sacks and clothing. It was difficult to sleep even though we were exhausted after a hard day's work, but I would often spend hours scratching and searching my clothes for fleas. The little buggers would get into the lining and were difficult to find. Often you would hear a crack, then a shout, 'got you, you bastard,' as another flea bit the dust. One of the best ways of getting rid of fleas was to hang your clothes outside at night in the freezing cold and by morning they would all have dropped off, but of course you had an icy shirt to put on when you got up. These bugs also caused infections and, with almost no drugs or medicines, many of us suffered greatly from the effects of these horrible little creatures. Not for the first time our medical officers did a wonderful job under very trying and difficult circumstances.

It was not surprising that in these dreadful, cold and damp conditions, pneumonia should be endemic amongst the men. The long nights were sheer hell, as men coughed up their lungs all down the hut. Quite a few of our lads died from pneumonia during that bitter winter and their bodies were cremated in a charnel house used for Japanese burials. It was almost impossible to sleep with the coughing, made even more difficult by one soldier in particular who kept singing over and over again a song from the 1930s called 'Lights out sweetheart, another weary day is through'. Someone would shout to him; 'If you don't shut up I'll put your f**king lights out'. Sometimes fights would break out over such issues as men's nerves and bodies were stretched to the limits. When fights broke out the guards would rush into the hut and start to bash the first man they came across (it was hard luck if you slept near the door) shouting 'all English soldier no pucking good ka. All men *no michi michi asta* (no food tomorrow).' 'We'll not miss much then,' I would mutter under my breath, as the staple diet was a small portion of rice sweepings with soya beans if you were lucky. Occasionally they would put waterlily stems in with the rice, they gave it a purple colour but it was equally tasteless. We named the rice and water lily mixture 'The Purple Death.'

Otani ruled his workforce with an iron fist, even the local workers hated him and they tried everything in the book to keep out of his way. He was a comical figure as he strode around with his cauliflower ear, wearing the usual Japanese *puttees*. Every morning at about 0800 hrs he would stride up the middle of the factory with his henchmen on either side. Everyone would be working away furiously but as soon as he left they eased off and did as little as possible. Each day during the winter months, before starting work the Japanese workers would fill buckets with wood, set them alight and squat around them to keep warm. We would join them getting as close as possible to the braziers as it was extremely cold: of course the factory would fill very quickly with thick smoke and noxious fumes. Not that this bothered any of us as keeping warm was a priority. One morning we were sat around a bucket rubbing our hands when Otani and his bully boys appeared. They were earlier than usual and caught us off guard. 'It's Otani,' I whispered to Mick and we quickly disappeared behind one of the large machines. Otani made a beeline for the buckets, kicked them all over, started screaming and shouting at the workers and chased them back to their machines; it really was quite an amusing sight. As soon as he left, they gathered up the buckets, refilled them and set them alight again.

We were marched back to camp each day at around 1300 hrs for our lunch. This usually consisted of a small amount of rice mixed with seaweed, oats and barley – not a very appetising dish after a hard morning's work. The local workers were also very poorly treated and fed very badly. Before they started work each day they would take off their hats, face the sun and pray that their machines would not break down; if a machine broke down the factory would lose production and they would incur the wrath of Mr Otani, even if it wasn't their fault. At the end of each working week they had to stand by their machines until Otani gave them permission to leave. He would come out of his office and give them all some potatoes and seaweed before dismissing them. Once when this procedure was taking place one of our lads shouted out, 'There would be a f**king row if I gave my missus potatoes and seaweed on a Friday night for a week's work.'

Work in the factory was hard. Christmas was just around the corner and food was scarce, but of course the Japanese blamed this on the Americans who were blockading the country and preventing imports. They also took out their frustrations and revenge on us, and we in turn stuck to our own little groups even more. As we walked to the factory one morning I saw a potato on the ground. Before I had a chance to bend down and grab it, a man we called the Professor beat me to it. The Professor was a real loner and never mixed with other POWs. We were of the opinion that this was because he was not a military man like the rest of us and had been a Professor of Music at the University of Kuala Lumpur before the Japanese invasion of Malaya. He was a very intelligent man and was suffering very badly under this harsh regime. It was a great shame that his undoubted talents went to waste for the three and a half years of his captivity, but life was so harsh for all of us that we had little time for sympathy.

One day whilst loading pig-iron into one of the trucks, the back of my neck felt sore every time the sack I was wearing touched it. I had become used to pain and suffering during the previous three years so initially I ignored it, but over the next couple of days it got considerably worse and a carbuncle began to develop causing me great pain. It became so bad that there was no alternative but to join the sick parade one day after work. The excellent Doctor Leadbetter was attending to many men suffering with a variety of ailments and diseases and when my turn came to be seen he examined it carefully.

'It isn't right for cutting yet, Corporal Wyatt,' he said.

'I'm in a great deal of pain Doctor. Can you not cut it now?' I moaned.

'OK corporal, we'll get it done. Bend over.'

As he slit the offending carbuncle I could feel the skin split and the puss run down the back of my neck. We had no local anaesthetics or painkillers of any kind but at least I would be rid of the gnawing, nagging pain that had been with me for days. With no bandages available, the doctor sent me to the Japanese medical orderlies who looked after the workers in the factory to try and get me bandaged up. They all pulled faces when they saw the state of my neck and refused to dress it, except for one wonderful lady who stepped forward and said she would do it for me. As she was bandaging me she said in a low voice, 'Me Christian.' She did a wonderful job and when she finished I thanked her profusely and wished her good luck for the future.

Many of the boys succumbed to pneumonia or pleurisy during this particularly cold Christmas and along with a return of beriberi (due to the poor diet) sadly several passed away. It was to our advantage that this bad period in the camp came at the same time as a high-ranking Japanese commander paid us a visit. Our officers demanded that the Red Cross food parcels, which we knew the Japanese held, should be given to us and he promised that he would do his best to arrange this before he left.

It was now January 1945 and Mick and I were delegated to work outside in the snow. At least in the factory we had some protection from the elements but we were now exposed to the full venom of a harsh Japanese winter. It was incredibly cold and bitter winds blew in from the sea. After a few days working under the most horrendous conditions I began to shiver uncontrollably.

'Better get you inside, Johnny,' Mick said. When the guards' backs were turned, he smuggled me back inside the factory where I found a warm post in a corner to curl up by, whilst Mick kept a look-out for the guards until it was time to return to camp. Doctor Leadbetter confirmed that I had developed pneumonia.

'Take this blanket, go to your bed space and don't get up until I tell you. I'll tell them that you are too ill to work,' he said.

For two weeks I lay in my filthy bug infested bed, shivering and sweating profusely and feeling as though the end of my life was near once again. But for the past three years I had been convinced that someone was watching over me, and this conviction was reinforced when, a few days later, a batch of Red Cross parcels arrived, probably the ones that the Japanese Commander had promised us just after Christmas. They contained some medicines including life-saving M and B tablets which the Doc insisted I took right away. The tablets did the trick and a few days later I was well enough to go back to work, thanks to my guardian angel. Each man was given a whole box to himself, minus any medical supplies which the Doc kept to use for the most severe cases. It was an amazing sight when we returned home after work one day to find the boxes waiting for us. The lads just went wild, just like when we opened our Christmas presents as children. It didn't matter that they were dated 1943 as they contained tins of meat, powdered milk and butter amongst other goodies. Many wept openly as they handled tins with English wrappers, not seen for nearly three years.

Life in Otani's factory was not without its funnier moments. One day Mick and I were ordered to push a truck loaded with pig-iron to a furnace. We pushed and shoved as hard as we could but it was too heavy for us and wouldn't budge so the *Hancho* ordered a woman worker to help us. She was in the middle, with Mick and I on either side, and every time we strained to push she kept farting.

'Was that you, Johnny?' said Mick.

'I only wish I could do that Mick, it must have been her,' I whispered, and we both burst out laughing. The woman then collapsed on the floor and when I drew the *Hancho's* attention he just walked over, put his foot on her and walked away. They often treated their own workers as badly as they treated us. This particular *Hancho*, who we nicknamed Tarzan because of his broad shoulders, was a nasty piece of work. Even the local workers kept out of his way. He would often just lash out at you as he passed by, always for no particular reason.

As the days dragged by we began to get more and more depressed by our terrible situation and I often wondered when and indeed if, it was all going to end. Occasionally we would get a boost when another batch of Red Cross parcels arrived. One day when we got back to camp we found them neatly stacked on our bed spaces. The Japanese had helped themselves to some of the contents, but they still contained chocolate, butter, milk powder, cigarettes and Marmite. Doctor Leadbetter took all the Marmite to give to the sick as they were in the most need of it. As I unpacked the chocolate I shed a tear as I visualised the lady who had packed them, far away in a civilised world. I knew we were out of sight but not out of mind.

The following day we trudged to work in a much happier mood, our spirits lifted by the contents of the latest Red Cross parcels. Whilst waiting for the truck to come back from unloading later that day, I was resting against a wall when suddenly without warning the whole factory began to rock violently. I felt dizzy and my stomach began to turn over. Looking up I saw the overhead cranes and cables swinging alarmingly from side to side. There were blue flashes everywhere and the ground started heaving under my feet. 'Earthquake!' someone shouted. Everyone started to run around in a state of panic. Many headed towards the canal with the intention of throwing themselves in to try and avoid the falling chimneys and overhead cables. The canal itself started to froth and bubble and the boats began to roll and toss around violently. Mick and I huddled together on an open bit of land whilst the ground groaned and shuddered beneath us. My first thoughts were that I had come through all the horrors of the death railway and the rat ridden hell ships, only to die in an earthquake in Japan. Fortunately after a few minutes the quake subsided and we all breathed a huge sigh of relief. I was unable to sleep that evening constantly thinking about that terrifying experience earlier, and when the camp was rocked by a second shock around midnight, my stomach turned over again. The hut started to creak and groan and I rolled from one side of my bed to the other, but whilst it was still an unnerving experience, I was not as frightened as earlier in the day. After about a minute or so the ground became still again.

When we arrived at the factory the next morning the sight that greeted us was one of desolation and destruction. It was low tide and the canal was a sea of mud and litter, and dead fish lay scattered everywhere. Much of the machinery was damaged and we had the unenviable task of cleaning everything up.

A few days later news started filtering through about the progress of the war in Europe. Fortunately one of the POWs who had lived in Hong Kong before the war had learnt some basic Japanese and was able to translate bits of local newspapers. We were asked by Regimental Sergeant Major Hastain, who was in charge of our hut, to steal some papers from the civilian workers at the factory. I would sometimes pinch a paper out of the back pockets of their coats, which they left hanging up near their machines, and stuff it under my shirt. In one we found out that the Americans were re-taking many of the islands around Japan and were closing in on Japan itself. We owed a lot to the man who translated them and kept us supplied with news: if he had been caught he would have been tortured by the dreaded Kempeitai.

It must have been around the middle of March when the Americans launched a massive bombing attack on Osaka. I heard the cry go up from the Japanese '*B Nee Ju Ku*' (Boeing 29s) a plane that they feared. Looking up I saw a great formation of B29s flying over like a flock of silver swans. Japanese fighter planes tried to intercept them but could not reach the altitude of the B29s and gave up the chase. With the capture of the Mariannas, the Americans now had a base at Saipan from which to launch their bombing raids; this gave us great hope that the Allies would soon win the war and we might at last be freed.

Our camp and the factory were hit by bombs dropped by the Americans and the sky all around was lit up in a fiery red glow from the many fires started by incendiary bombs. Parts of the camp were badly damaged and all that was left of our place of 'employment' were the toilets. A thick pallor of smoke hung over the whole area and it was difficult to see more than a couple of hundred yards. It seemed as though all of Japan was burning. I had seen the London Blitz back in September 1940 but to me that was nothing compared with what I was now witnessing: all around us, factories, houses and shops seemed to be on fire. The raid went on for more than twenty-four hours and I felt certain at that point that the war would soon be over. I just prayed to God that they would not kill me before I had the chance to go home and, as usual, he answered my prayers.

A day or so later a squadron of American B52s came over and we all ran for cover as they machine-gunned the camp. I could clearly see the faces of the pilots in their cockpits and although I was worried about being hit, I was only too pleased to see the Yanks as I knew that, at last, victory was in sight. Rumour had it that they were from a big American fleet just a few hundred miles off the coast of Japan and that an invasion was imminent. When these planes swooped over the camp the guards immediately fled, leaving us to our own fate from the attacking aircraft. There was no water or electricity and what food left in the stores had been set alight by the cannon fire. The smoke haze was so bad that it blocked out the sun and my eyes stung and watered constantly. It was at this time that Mick took ill and was admitted to the camp hospital. I was very concerned about him and took him some of my food each day to try and build him up.

When the raids ceased the Japanese returned, but there was no work for us to do as the factory was in ruins. The Camp Commandant Warrant Officer Mitsuzo Inagaki said that, 'You POWs must *worko* somewhere else.' During our time in Amagasaki Camp, Japanese guards came and went on a regular basis but we were mainly guarded by Sergeant Yoshinari Mimemoto, Sergeant Hajime Kakuta, Corporal Hiroichi Uno, Corporal Toshihira Fukada and First Lieutenant Toshio Mori.

On 17 June we were ordered to pack our belongings and be ready to move out. I was devastated when I was told that Mick was to stay behind in the camp hospital to recuperate and there were tears in my eyes when I said to goodbye to my best mate. I really felt that I would never see him again.

We left the camp and marched along through the streets of Amagasaki towards the railway station. As we strode along with our heads held high, the devastation caused by the American bombs was evident. Houses and shops were in ruins and it appeared as though a giant had dropped handfuls of pebbles over the city from a great height. It was a bitter-sweet experience as it signified that perhaps the war was coming to a close, but of course as we were the enemy in their land, we were fearful for our lives. People lined the roads as we tramped on, throwing stones and bits of wood at us and shaking their fists in anger, as though it had been us who had bombed their homes.

It was deathly quiet when we reached the station and we waited patiently on the deserted platform for a couple of hours until eventually a train came along and we were herded aboard. Our destination was a mystery, but as we sat on the platform the guards came round with cardboard boxes containing oats and barley. The sun was just beginning to set as we pulled out of the station and we settled down, in reasonable comfort, on the bench seats to get some much needed sleep. I dozed on and off for most of the night and had no idea where we were going, or in which direction, until the sun rose the next morning. We were travelling in a north-easterly direction, and for several hours the train passed through some delightful mountainous scenery. It eventually stopped at the station of Toyama on the other side of Honshu Island near a sheltered bay, where another small electric local train was waiting for us. In a matter of minutes we had disembarked and boarded the smaller train bound for our new camp number nine Nagoya, at a place called Ohirota near the docks.

Nagoya Camp had just been opened a few weeks before we arrived and was much better than the previous one at Amagasaki. It had previously been a barracks for civilian labourers and was situated in the middle of some fields. Some of the original buildings had been repaired and additional ones built of wood: the whole camp was surrounded by a fence ten feet tall. Around 230 Americans, a few Australians and couple of Dutchmen were already there when we arrived and they made us 'Limeys' very welcome. Most of them had been taken prisoner on the Philippines or from the Bataan campaign with a few from Wake Island. The camp was commanded by two American Officers and they were happy to give us the responsibility for running our own affairs. For some reason Doctor Leadbetter was not sent with us to Nagoya but fortunately there was an excellent American doctor in the camp called Lieutenant Brown.

Although Nagoya camp was a lot better than the previous one we had been in, we were still troubled by fleas. By now it was the height of summer and dozens of them found their way into your clothes and bedding and indeed into every other nook and cranny presented to them. The little buggers made our lives a misery and I would often spend half the night cracking them between my thumbnails. We worked for the Nippon Tsuun Company unloading ships which were bringing in cement, coal, timber and beans. Work was hard, the days long and the only food we got was rice and soya beans twice a day. Many of the boys were in a bad state by now. If you could not work – you got no food. 'No worko, no *michi – michi*' (rice) they said over and over again.

The Japanese officer in charge of the camp was called Seiichi Furiyama, but we saw little of him as one of his minions seemed to take care of all the day to day dealings with the POWs. We nicknamed him the 'One-armed bandit' as he had lost an arm fighting in China. He looked a right clown and carried a sword in a scabbard which trailed along on the ground behind him when he walked. Each morning he would come through our hut shouting '*Shigoto – Shigoto*' (work) and if you didn't move quickly enough he would bash you with his scabbard. He was a right bastard. Once when we were marching back from working on the docks, the guard saw one of the Americans smoking, which was forbidden. The Yank threw his butt away before the guards could see who it was but they stopped us, lined us up and demanded to know who was smoking. No one would own up so they kept us standing there for what seemed like hours. I was so hungry and tired, and just to get the ordeal over, although I wasn't a smoker, I said, 'Me smoko.' The guard called me out and gave me a punch under the chin. Had I not owned up we would probably have been there all night long; when we got back to the camp I never even got a 'thank you' from the Yanks.

For the first couple of weeks in Nagoya, it was a relief to be free from the wailing air-raid sirens, but at the beginning of July the B29s started to attack the docks where we worked. We were then ordered to build air raid shelters for ourselves and set to work immediately, digging up most of the open space in camp. We were fortunate to obtain a good supply of wood from nearby and we were able to dive into our 'bolt-holes' when the B29s came over again.

These attacks went on for nearly a month and at the beginning of August the town of Toyama was completely devastated by an air raid. The inhabitants had been warned of the attacks a couple of days before, by leaflets dropped from Allied planes, and indeed many of them vanished into the surrounding mountains. As we were only a couple of miles from the town, we had a good view of the inferno. Huge clouds of smoke and sparks blew over the camp and at one stage we thought we might have to be evacuated; the camp gates were opened by the guards and we were just waiting for the order to run to the nearby paddy fields.

Chapter 10

The Japanese Surrender

The Nazis had been defeated in Europe by this time but we were not aware of this, so routine at the camp carried on as normal. Although we did notice a gradual change in the attitude of the locals; one schoolteacher told her children to throw stones at us as we marched past the school each day. They also drew their hands across their throats and made hanging signs as we passed by. Supplies of food were beginning to run out and we were starving, as were the local Japanese population. The situation was getting desperate and I began to despair once more about ever seeing home and my family.

The camp was always alive with rumours. The biggest one doing the rounds was that that there had been a big bombing raid on the city of Hiroshima, some 300 miles away, causing great devastation. Little did we know that this rumour was indeed true and that the Americans had dropped the first ever atomic bomb on the city. The dropping of this bomb on Hiroshima turned out to be one of the most important and historic events in the history of mankind, and an event that was to save my life and the lives of thousands of my colleagues in the Far East. Here was I, sitting in a POW camp in Japan, not more than 300 miles from where history was made on 6 August 1945.

Four or five days later, as we were trudging wearily to work, we passed a group of Americans who shouted over to us:

'Put those shovels down, Limeys, it's these bastards' turn now. You're free.'

We trudged on, not daring to believe them, as there had been many rumours about the war ending during the past few months and each had been baseless. But when we got back to camp at the end of the day, we realised that there must be something in it. There were no more shouts of '*Shigoto – shigoto*' from our guards, and they suddenly declared that the next day would be a '*yasume*' day. Maybe the Yanks were right and for the first time during my captivity I really began to believe that war might be over. '*Yasume*' day meant we would be allowed to have a bath, another indication that something was happening as baths had became somewhat of a rarity in recent months (due to the shortage of fuel). They also told us that we could arrange some sports activities, again an indication that attitudes were changing.

That night the hut was alive with whispered conversations as we discussed the possibility that the Yanks might be right. It was just about impossible to get any sleep, but we still realised that our lives might be in danger. There had been much talk over the past few months about a rumoured death warrant, issued by the Japanese high command, for all POWs if the homelands were invaded. Although we were not aware of it at the time, the Japanese had formally agreed to surrender on 10 August, and back home Prime Minister Clement Attlee declared the following two days as national holidays.

It was a real treat to not have to get up to go to work the next day and I relaxed in my bed space listening to some Japanese martial music coming from one of the guard's radios. Suddenly the music was interrupted and the Japanese national anthem was played. This was followed by a very slow, sober speech in Japanese. I sprang out of my bed space and ran outside to witness the guards springing to attention and shouting the usual 'hi hi'. When the speech finished, they bowed towards the radio, presented arms and promptly disappeared. POWs came streaming out of their huts and word spread quickly, via one of our interpreters, that Emperor Hirohito had just told the nation that the war was over.

Many years later I came across an English transcript of the Emperor's speech that emotional day on 15 August 1945:

'After pondering deeply the general trends of the world and the actual conditions obtaining in our empire today, we have decided to effect a settlement of the present situation by resorting to an extraordinary measure.

We have ordered our Government to communicate to the governments of the United States, Great Britain, China and the Soviet Union that our empire accepts the provisions of their joint declaration.

To strive for the common prosperity and happiness of all nations as well as the security and well-being of our subjects is the solemn obligation which has been handed down by our imperial ancestors and which we lay close to the heart.

Indeed we declared war on America and Britain out of our sincere desire to ensure Japan's self-preservation and the stabilisation of South East Asia, it being far from our thought either to infringe upon the sovereignty of other nations or to embark upon territorial aggrandizement.

But now the war has lasted for nearly four years, despite the best that has been done by everyone – the gallant fighting of the military and naval forces, the diligence and assiduity of our servants of the state and the devoted service of our 100,000,000 people – the war situation has developed not necessarily to Japan's advantage while the general trends of the world have turned against her interest.

Moreover, the enemy has begun to employ a new and most cruel bomb, the power of which to do damage, is indeed incalculable, taking the toll of innocent lives. Should we continue to fight, it would not only result in an ultimate collapse and the obliteration of the Japanese nation, but also it would lead to the total extinction of human civilisation.

Such being the case, how are we to save the millions of our subjects, or to atone ourselves before the hallowed spirits of our imperial ancestors? This is the reason why we have ordered the acceptance of the provisions of the joint declaration of the powers.

We cannot but express the deepest sense of regret to our allied nations of South East Asia, who have consistently cooperated with the Empire towards the emancipation of East Asia.

The thoughts of those officers and men as well as others who have fallen in the fields of battle. Those who have died at their posts of duty, or those who met with death (otherwise) and all their bereaved families, pains our heart night and day.

The welfare of the wounded and the war sufferers and of those who have lost their homes and livelihood is the object of our profound solicitude. The hardships and suffering to which our nation is to be subjected hereafter will be certainly great.

We are keenly aware of the inmost feelings of all of you, our subjects. However it is according to the dictates of time and fate that we have resolved to pave the way for a grand peace for all the generations to come by enduring the (unavoidable) and suffering what is insufferable. Having been able to save face and maintain the structure of the Imperial State, we are always with you, our good and loyal subjects, relying upon your sincerity and integrity.

Beware most strictly of any outbursts of emotion that may engender needless complications, of any fraternal contention and strife that may create confusion, lead you astray and cause you to lose the confidence of the world.

Let the entire nation continue as one family from generation to generation, ever firm in its faith of the imperishableness of its divine land, and mindful of its heavy burdens of responsibilities, and the long road before it. Unite your total strength to be devoted to the construction of the future. Cultivate the ways of rectitude, nobility of spirit, and work with resolution so that you may enhance the innate glory of the Imperial State and keep pace with the progress of the world.'

As we stood in small groups around the camp dumfounded by this wonderful news, our officers came over to each group and ordered us to form up in front of the huts. We were to be addressed by the Japanese Camp Commandant, Captain Kubo. The One-armed-Bandit, as we called Kudo, then stood up on a small platform and said to us in broken English: 'All waru pinish, u men to Englando.' He was closely followed by an interpreter who calmly informed us that: 'Two huge bombs had been dropped killing many Japanese people, the

Imperial Japanese Army had surrendered and we were free to return home. It is very bad; Japan is appealing to the United Nations.'

As Kudo and the interpreter walked away there was a stunned silence amongst the ranks of emaciated men. My mind was in a whirl. After nearly four years of hell it dawned on me that maybe I might just see my family again. But even now any thought of returning home was dismissed; my hopes of survival had been dashed so many times that I simply refused to believe these men for whom I held such hate. It was only when the Camp CO stood up and confirmed that the war was over and we would soon be going home, that I could really believe it.

Suddenly all hell broke loose. We hugged each other, dropped on our knees and said the Lord's Prayer. Some of the men were shouting. Some were crying. Some didn't move at all. Some seemed stunned and those left in the huts, too weak to move, just lay there staring up at the ceiling. We were indeed going home. Then an American doctor stood up and brought us back to good order and said: 'Men, your freedom is here. You have suffered much but I beg of you all, do not go out looking for revenge: one bullet or bayonet through you and all the horrors you have suffered will be in vain.'

I am certain that if the war had not ended when it did more than half of the POWs in Japan would have died of extreme starvation or hypothermia during the coming winter.

Over the next few days excitement amongst the lads began to mount, we were impatient to get out of the camp and be on our way home. Our officers ordered us to sit tight and wait for further instructions as the job of repatriating thousands of POWs from all over the Far East was no easy task. It was a difficult time for us as, technically, we were now free men but we were marooned in a country that had just been brought to its knees by the Allies.

We were ordered to paint the roofs of our huts yellow, with the letters POW in black so that they could be seen from the air to assist with food drops. We went about this task with great enthusiasm and waited with our tongues hanging out for the goodies to drop from the sky. Sure enough early the next morning American planes swooped over the camp and parachutes of red, white and blue floated down with large boxes swinging underneath. It was a wonderful feeling when the whole camp rushed out to collect this 'manna from heaven.' In his excitement one of the boys failed to keep looking up and got hit by one of the falling boxes. His injuries were minor however and he was soon back with the rest of us collecting the goodies. Many of the boxes split open on impact with the ground, and we ran from box to box like children at Christmas, picking up armfuls of food and other luxuries. It had been three and a half years since we had seen food in such quantity and we were like vultures swooping down on their prey.

I collected as much as I could and ran back to the hut to stash my 'booty' under my bed before dashing back for the next lot. The boxes contained chocolate, bread, butter, milk, tea, Bovril and all sorts of other foodstuffs; I was plunged from hell into heaven in a matter of minutes. Just as we were about to taste the fruits of our labours an American doctor gave us a stern warning:

'Don't eat too much food all at once men, your stomachs are not used to such rich food and you will become ill.' 'Stuff that, I'm starving, I don't care if I'm sick,' I said, as I tucked into the food with gusto. When you had been starved for three and a half years and all this food started raining down on you it was impossible to resist gorging yourself. It was difficult to sleep that night as my stomach was so full and my mind was working overtime. I was just so happy to have survived the last three and a half years of hell: sleep seemed be a waste of my time as a free man again.

For the next three weeks we idled our time away, waiting for the order to move out. Although we were more comfortable than we had been for three and a half years and had plenty of food, it was a most frustrating time waiting to set off for home. It was wonderful to hear reveille sounded each morning and the roll-call in English instead of Japanese. The guards were also ordered not to attend morning and evening parades. It was truly uplifting to have freedom and control over our lives again.

Chapter 11

Homeward Bound

It was 5 September 1945, almost a month after the atomic bomb had been dropped on Hiroshoma, when we marched out of the gates of the camp for the final time. Not with the usual feeling of depression and dread about the grind of the day to follow, but with a feeling of unbelievable elation that it was really all over.

We sang and cheered as we marched about two miles along the road towards the small local railway station, waving our home-made Union Jacks and shouting to the Japanese people as they peered out at us from behind dirty, broken windows. The strain of the past months was evident on their gaunt faces, as they tried to come to terms with the great disaster that had befallen their nation, and of course we held our heads high with the pride of a nation that had won a war.

At the station we were quickly loaded onto a train and soon we were on our way out of Nagoya. The city had been badly hit by American bombing raids and all that was left of the great factories and industrial areas were the smoking charred wrecks of burnt out buildings. It was a pitiful sight, but I felt nothing for the Japanese people after the suffering and hardship that their army had imposed on me for the past three and a half years.

It was around four in the morning when the train finally pulled into Shizuoka station. We were looking forward to getting out and stretching our legs but we were instructed by the officers not to leave the carriages as this was only a very short stop before heading on towards our final destination, the Port of Yokosuka, another two hours away. Dawn was just breaking when the train finally pulled up alongside the docks at Yokosuka and it was a great relief to finally leave the cramped carriages and stretch our legs. As we chatted and joked on the dock side, the sight of so many Allied ships lying just outside the port was one of the most uplifting and wonderful feelings of my life. For the past few weeks I'd felt as though I was dreamimg and would suddenly wake up to the squalor and ill-treatment of a Japanese POW camp once more, but the sight of these majestic warships was certainly very real.

We had not long to wait before a small armada of barges came chugging into the harbour and pulled up alongside the quayside. 'Jump aboard buddy,' shouted one of the smartly dressed American sailors. I didn't need a second invitation and gratefully hopped into the barge, followed by dozens of eager and excited POWs. Within minutes the barge was on its way out of the harbour and heading towards a large American hospital ship sat at anchor just offshore. As we neared the ship hundreds of sailors lined the upper decks waving to us and of course we all waved back furiously. The name USS *Benevolence* was emblazoned on the hull and it had two huge red crosses painted on its side. What a comforting sight those three words were – United States Ship – the first time in three and half years we'd seen a friendly vessel.

As we clambered aboard we were greeted by the first white women we had seen since we'd left Britain: American nurses in their clean white uniforms. They looked to me just like beautiful angels and I think I fell in love with each and every one of them as they made us feel so welcome. It was like arriving at the Promised Land after nearly four years in the depths of hell. Our old clothes were taken from us and immediately thrown overboard. It was a great feeling to see those horrible smelly clothes float away out to sea, and to soak under a hot shower for the first time in months.

The Medical Officers on the ship were very concerned about any diseases we might be carrying and after a thorough medical examination; we were given the most modern drugs available at that time. Although we felt like 'lepers' at first, we were delighted to be receiving the best medical treatment. My malaria was treated with a drug called Atebrin and I was quickly feeling on top of the world again.

The *Benevolence* was a wonderful ship. It was just over a year old, having been launched on the 10 July 1944 and transferred to the American Navy as a hospital ship three weeks later. It arrived in Japanese waters on 20 August 1944 as part of the main American force, for what were to be the final strikes on Japan. With the dropping of the bombs the ship was transferred to the duties of caring for POWs like ourselves. It was now the 12 September and whilst we were receiving wonderful treatment from the Americans, the Japanese were formally surrendering back in Singapore to Lord Mountbatten. (Copy of the official signed surrender document is attached in Appendix 2.)

After a few days we were transferred to an American aircraft carrier, the USS *Wagner,* lying a few hundred yards away. The generosity on board the *Wagner* knew no bounds, everything was free: chocolate, cigarettes and ice cream were in big demand and we were given a chitty that entitled us to go anywhere on the ship and order anything we liked from the messes. The *Wagner* took us from Tokyo Bay to the Philippines where we were taken ashore and transported to a large holding camp about eleven miles outside the city. The camp was administered by the Australians and here we were kitted out in new regimental shirts and shorts by the ladies from the Women's Volunteer Force. They even pressed our clothes and sewed on our chevrons. I began to feel like a soldier again for the first time in so many years. We then spent a couple of very frustrating weeks in Manila (we all just wanted to get home as soon a possible) but the hospitality and the wonderful scenery made up for some of this frustration.

On 24 September we boarded the 22,000 ton American transport ship the USS *Admiral Charles Hughes* which was to take us on the 7,000 mile voyage across the Pacific to San Francisco on the next leg of our long journey back to England. With over 3,000 passengers on board, many of whom were American servicemen returning home from the war, the *Hughes* upped anchor on 24 September 1945 and steamed out into the Pacific at a steady fifteen knots. Once again the hospitality of the Americans was of the first order – we wanted for nothing. The ship had a cinema and a theatre: we had unlimited access to recently released films and superb stage shows. The voyage across the Pacific lasted around two weeks. I enjoyed the complete sense of relaxation as the ship ploughed through the crystal clear waters; I spent hours just sitting in deckchairs on the boat deck, daydreaming and chatting with the other lads about what we were going to do when we got home.

As the ship sailed past Honolulu, word spread around that plans had been changed and we would now be heading for Seattle, Washington. Somehow it did not matter to us as we were so content on board the *Hughes* that anywhere in the United States would do. A week or so later, as we approached the West coast of the United States, plans were changed again and the ship headed up the coast towards our new destination of Victoria, Vancouver Island in Canada. The Americans on board were most upset about all these changes but most people were just glad to be getting somewhere near home after so many years away.

Dawn was breaking on 9 October when we steamed into the Juan de Fuca Strait and around the southern tip of Vancouver Island towards the most southern city in Canada, Victoria. The scenery along the coastline was stunning and I spent most of the morning leaning over the port rails gazing at my first sight of an English speaking country for more than three years. I just couldn't wait to get ashore. Rounding the headland the grand city of Victoria opened up before us. It was difficult to get a space on the rails as the decks we so crowded with soldiers just gazing in silent awe at their first sight of Canada.

As the ship slowly made its way into the British Naval Base at Esquimalt, hundreds of small ships surrounded us, each with sirens and hooters sounding a glorious welcome. The silent awe gradually turned into a crescendo of noise as we all started cheering and waving at the small ships and to the hundreds of people who lined the quayside as we approached our berth. As we drew alongside the quay the sight of hundreds of people waving flags and cheering made us feel like celebrities, I just felt so proud to be British and couldn't stop waving back to these wonderful friendly people. It was 1430 hrs when we eventually tied up at the quayside, exactly the time we were scheduled to arrive.

The Canadians showered us with gifts of fruit, cigarettes and other luxury items when we alighted – it was truly humbling and I felt really honoured to be accepted by these great people. Our kitbags were taken from us and before long we were boarding waiting coaches to take us to the camp accommodation laid on by our hosts. At the camp there was a Red Cross canteen where we were able to get as much food as we wanted and the Red Cross ladies even sewed our numerals and ribbons onto the new uniforms we had been issued.

Although I was missing my mate Mick, it wasn't long before I found a new mate in another Irishman called Paddy Coughlan. Paddy was a real charmer with the girls and we got friendly with a couple of Canadian girls who really took a fancy to us. I envied the way he was always so at ease with the girls, and of course his Irish blarney helped. But I felt embarrassed and tongue-tied when we were with them – three and a half years in the company of only men had taken its toll. There were so many available Canadian girls around Victoria that quite a few of the boys decided to stay, many of them marrying local girls.

After about a week in Victoria those of us who had decided to head on home were ordered down to Esquimalt to board the paddle steamer *Princess Charlotte* for the next leg of the journey up to the city of Vancouver. The journey took only a few hours and it was most pleasant to watch the wonderful scenery of Vancouver Island passing by on our port side. At Vancouver we boarded a Pullman train of the Canadian National Railroad service for the 3,000 mile journey across Canada, the longest single train journey in the world. For five days and nights we passed through some of the most wonderful and breathtaking scenery I had ever seen. This most wonderful of journeys was made even more agreeable by the polite and friendly Canadian train staff who took care of our every need. The rugged beauty of the Rocky Mountains took my breath away as they flashed past the windows of the train. We stopped briefly at the city of Calgary, before heading on through the exotic sounding towns of Medicine Hat and Moose Jaw, towards the great lakes and the east coast.

Soon the train was chugging along near to Lake Superior heading for our next stopping off point, the great city of Winnipeg, the capital of Manitoba. When we pulled slowly into Winnipeg railway station the sight that met our eyes was quite amazing. It seemed like most of the city was on the platform waving and cheering and the local brass band were playing. After an hour or so to stretch our legs, we boarded the train again and headed east toward Halifax, Nova Scotia, where we were to embark on the final leg of our long journey home.

As the train pulled into Halifax, the sight of the *Queen Elizabeth* lying alongside the docks was one of the most uplifting sights of my life. It signified everything about good old England and I knew then that home was near; we were about to board the largest passenger ship ever built up to that time. We wasted little time getting off the train and were immediately ushered on board. As I walked along the deck towards the cabins we had been allocated I felt a tap on the shoulder: 'Oi, Johnny, how are you?' I recognised the voice immediately; it was my old mate Mick Shiels and we embraced each other again. We hadn't seen each other for four months, but it seemed that we were destined to be together again at the end of our epic experience.

Soon the *Queen Elizabeth* slipped her moorings and glided slowly out of Halifax Harbour into the cold grey North Atlantic. Somehow this was the most poignant moment for Mick and I: we knew that the next time we stepped ashore it would be on British soil, after nearly six years away from our families.

The five day journey across the Atlantic was smooth and uneventful. We idled the time away chatting, playing cards and walking around the deck of the vast liner. When news spread through the ship that we were approaching the tip of Cornwall and the entrance to the English Channel, we all rushed back on deck to get our first sight of 'England's green and pleasant land'. It was a typical dark and damp December day so we saw nothing until we edged into the Solent and tied up alongside the docks in Southampton. This was the last time the *Queen Elizabeth* would cross the oceans carrying troops back from World War Two; it had been in military service since 1940 and would soon resume its career as a luxury cruise liner.

Chapter 12

Home Sweet Home

We arrived in Southampton on 4 December 1945, almost six years to the day since I waved goodbye to my family as a fresh faced nineteen year old. I was now twenty-five and I felt as though I had left my youth behind in those stinking prison camps in the Far East. I was now an old man.

It was a truly emotional moment when I stepped off the gangplank of the *Queen Elizabeth* onto English soil again. I felt like getting down on my knees and kissing the ground, but before I had time to do it, we were ushered aboard a waiting bus and taken to a holding camp on the outskirts of the town. The camp was an old army drill hall where we spent one night on camp beds. The next day we were thoroughly debriefed about our experiences and checked over again by the Medical Officers. It was bitterly cold in the hall but I was just pleased to be back in good old England again. We were issued with a War Office document entitled 'To all British Army Ex-Prisoners of War', a copy of the King's message to all Japanese Prisoners of War (see Appendix 3) and a copy of a letter written to us from Colonel Foster the Commanding Officer of the East Surrey Regiment (See Appendix 4). We were also told that we would receive our back pay in the form of a cheque in a week or so and then allowed to make arrangements to go home on leave. I contacted my brother Jim and he arranged to get the train down to Southampton the next day.

The next morning I packed up my belongings and said goodbye to Mick. It was an emotional moment as we promised each other faithfully that we would keep in touch. 'Look after yourself, Johnny,' he said as we hugged emotionally. We both shed a tear as we parted and I have never forgotten those four poignant words spoken by a man who had stuck by me throughout during those difficult years as a POW.

Jim and I boarded the train at Southampton and soon we were chugging through the English countryside on the way up to London. I was excited about getting home, but as we neared the capital the sight of bomb-damaged buildings and the drab greyness of England depressed me, especially after witnessing the colourful scenery and sunshine of Canada. Barbed wire littered the countryside and on either side of the road concrete huts and air raid shelters made for a very dismal scene.

Mum, Dad, brother George and sister Doreen were all there to meet me when the train pulled into London Bridge station. The tears flowed freely as we hugged and kissed. I was home again in the arms of my family – a very emotional time for the Wyatts.

I was delighted that George had been married whilst I was away serving King and country. His wife Freda had given birth to a baby boy named Michael just six months before I got home and I was really looking forward to seeing my little nephew for the first time. On the way up from Southampton on the train Jim told me that the family were now living on the first and second floors of a new house in Abingdon Grove. This news was disappointing as I was looking forward to seeing the old house where I spent many happy days as a child but Jim told me that it had been bombed by the Germans and the family were forced to move.

On the journey home from America I had accumulated all sorts of luxuries; sweets, chocolates, cigarettes and many other small items which the family would not have been able to buy in post-war England because of the rationing still in place. When I tipped them all out of my kit bag onto the kitchen table their mouths opened wide with surprise, they had not seen such luxuries since before the war. It was a truly special day. The Wyatt family had strung banners all around the room with 'welcome home John' scrawled on them. My mother had planned a special celebratory chicken dinner that evening and as we sat around the dining table chatting and laughing, she asked me if I had received the Christmas pudding she sent out to me on 8

June 1941 along with a telegram. I never received the pudding but I have kept a copy of mum's telegram:

For Censorship Purposes

Please write your message below, with your full name and rank in block letters.

From: Mrs. L. Wyatt of 17 Maddin Road, Sydenham, SM 26

To: Her son Private John Wyatt

Hello John… Mum speaking. We're all well at home, and Aunt Mary, Aunt Nellie and Uncle Lou send love and best wishes to you. There's a Christmas parcel on the way with one of my puddings, so don't swallow the three penny piece.

We are so excited when we receive your letters, and the last one told us about the snake and the rat.

Keep smiling son. Every day is one day nearer. Cheerio and God bless you.

I was looking forward to seeing my girlfriend Elsie again, but was devastated when my mother told me that she had married another man during the time I was a POW.

'She married a marine John, and when I found out, I went round to her house and demanded your ring back. By that time she did not have it so I left empty handed,' Mum said.

Although things between Elsie and I were over, I felt that I just had to go and see her again, so the next morning I walked round to her house and nervously knocked on the door. She had heard that I was back and looked very sheepish when she opened the door.

'Hello Elsie, remember me,' I said, feeling rather foolish to even ask the question.

'Course I do John, let's go for a walk in the park,' she replied.

As we strolled through the park, Elsie broke down in tears.

'I'm really sorry John, but I heard from the authorities in 1942 that you were reported missing, possibly dead,' she sobbed.

'Don't cry Elsie, I fully understand the position you were in,' I said, struggling to hold back the tears myself.

'I'm not bitter, have no regrets and I'm only too pleased that you are happy. I'm just thankful to God that I have survived the horrors of the last four years.'

My heart was heavy as I walked home that day but there was nothing I could do about it so I just had to try and get on with my life.

It became very difficult for me to adapt to life back home in Sydenham and I began to feel trapped in that miserable house in Abingdon Grove. I had forgotten what life was like out of uniform and it was obvious that the previous four years' horrific experiences were still playing on my mind. Things weren't helped by the fact that the house was owned by a grumpy, miserable man who lived on the ground floor and constantly complained about the noise we were making. I felt very claustrophobic in that house, probably because I had spent the last three and a half years out of doors sleeping in large open huts with many other men. I could not get used to sleeping in a small room on my own and all I wanted to do was to get out in the fresh air and walk around. I was also not too keen on mixing with people and, of course, I had lost touch with most of my original friends. This suited me as I preferred my own company and of course many of my old mates had left the area anyway. One of my best friends, Fred Kenwood, sadly died in a German POW camp.

Most mornings I would leave the house after breakfast and walk for miles around the streets of Sydenham on my own. This was very therapeutic and my mother and father were sympathetic and understanding. They appreciated how I felt after the horrible experiences of the camps and just left me alone to try and put my life back in some sort of order. For the first few months I just couldn't settle down at all and felt very depressed. I made no effort to get a job and as my back Army pay was about £300 (quite a lot in those days) I was not short of money.

My brother Jim was still in the Fire Service and just before Christmas he said to me:

'Would you like to come over to New Cross Fire Station and talk to the lads, John?'

As I was feeling so down I was reluctant to even agree to Jim's invitation, but just to please him I agreed. A few days later I caught the no. 75 bus from Sydenham over to New Cross Fire Station where

Jim met me at the station entrance. He took me on a tour of the station, showed me around the appliances and introduced me to the lads on his shift and the girls manning the switchboard. The girls were really friendly and Jim said to me:

'Molly over there remembers you from before the war and would like to go out with you, John.'

This was the same girl who had met me in 1939 when I visited the station and who had always asked Jim how I was getting on. In 1942 he had been able to tell her that I was a Prisoner of War somewhere in the Far East as he had heard it on Vatican Radio.

'I'm pleased that he is still alive,' she had to him at the time.

Little did I know that this attractive Irish girl I first met at Perrivale Fire Station in 1940 was soon to become my wife.

I was quite embarrassed at this suggestion and turned beetroot red. I still felt uncomfortable in the presence of women after so many years surrounded by men in the POW camps, but when I looked across Molly was smiling at me. She was very attractive and I fell for her right away. We chatted briefly for a few minutes before I eventually plucked up the courage to invite her to the pictures that evening and from that day on Molly and I were hooked. I suppose I must have made some sort of impression on her back in 1940 and it wasn't long before we became besotted with each other. I would catch the bus over to New Cross to see her every other day and in the spring of 1946 I asked her to marry me. She had no hesitation in saying yes. We decided on Saturday, 4 August for our wedding day and of course there was always only going to be one choice for my best man – Mick Shiels. My brothers fully understood my reasons for asking Mick and I was delighted when he wrote back to me to accept.

August the fourth 1946 was probably the happiest day of my life, though the day I set foot back in England a year earlier might have been on a par with it. After the reception in Saint Philip's church hall in Shrewsbury Road, we left for a short honeymoon at a small place in Surrey called Shere, near Guildford. Ironically, Shere is just a couple of miles from the present East Surrey Museum in Clandon – well worth a visit if you are in the area. There was none of your fancy honeymoons to foreign sunspots at that time and of course I had seen enough of the sun to last me a lifetime.

Molly and I then settled down to married life living with my parents in Sydenham, but although I was happy to be married to the girl of my dreams, I was still unemployed and struggling to come to terms with life after my experiences in the Far East. The only jobs available at the time seemed to be in factories, but my fear of enclosed spaces prevented me from taking any of them and I continued to sign on the dole each week.

For the rest of 1946 and into 1947 I spent my days mooching around the streets. Jobs in the open air were hard to come by and the future looked bleak. Molly was still working at the Fire Station and with my dole money and Army back pay we were at least comfortably well-off. We were able to rent a house in Algiers Street and just before Easter 1947 we were absolutely delighted to discover that Molly was pregnant. We just couldn't wait until the baby was born. The next nine months flew past and on 13 January 1948 our lovely daughter Janet was born. Janet's birth brought a whole new meaning to my life and with plenty of time on my hands I enjoyed pushing the pram around the streets of Sydenham. For some of the time at least I was able to forget about the horrors of the Japanese Prisoner of War camps. Then, as 1948 drew to a close and the New Year dawned, I managed to get a job as a postman in Sydenham. It really was the best job for me as I could be out in the fresh air all day walking around – a job that I was very happy doing for the next thirty-seven years.

Three and a half years later the Wyatt family expanded to four when our second daughter Jane was born on 18 August 1951. I now had two wonderful little girls to push around the streets.

We led a very happy life for the next twenty-five years until my father died in 1975 followed by my mother ten years later, but watching our two daughters grow up, get married and have families was a great comfort to me. I was very contented walking the streets of Sydenham delivering post and meeting lots of nice people; slowly I was able to put the horrors of the POW camps to the back of my mind as I enjoyed my children and grandchildren. But, as all Japanese Prisoners of War will tell you, you are never able to forget, or in my case forgive. It was 1985 when I retired from the Post Office, after thirty-six years of delivering letters around my beloved Sydenham.

Conclusion

The fall of Malaya and Singapore to the Japanese on 15 February 1942 has often been labelled the British Empire's worst ever military defeat. Blame has been portioned out between Churchill: the Battalion Commanders in the field in Malaya and Singapore and ordinary soldiers like me. Churchill described the Fall of Singapore as 'a heavy and far-reaching military defeat' but the rest of the nation felt that it was utter humiliation. Three and a half weeks before the Japanese invaded Thailand and Malaya he announced to the war cabinet back in London that large-scale reinforcements would NOT be sent to Malaya. Britain and its allies were fighting a war on several fronts at the time and with the home lands under threat from the Nazis, he felt that the defence of British possessions in the Far East was not high on his priority list. In his memoirs he said:

> 'There was no way that Great Britain and the British Empire single handed could fight Germany, Italy and wage the Battle of Britain, the Battle of the Atlantic and the Battle of the Middle East. And at the same time stand thoroughly prepared in Burma, the Malay peninsula and generally in the Far East against the impact of a vast military empire like Japan with more than seventy mobile divisions, the third largest navy in the world, a great air force and the thrust of 80 – 90 warlike Asians. If we had started to scatter our forces over these immense areas in the Far East we would have been ruined.
>
> The Japanese mastery of the air in Malaya and Singapore, as has been described from our bitter needs elsewhere and for which the local commanders were in no way responsible, was another deadly fact.
>
> > (*The Second World War* by Winston Churchill –
> > Pimlico Books 2002)'

Churchill had been desperately trying to persuade President Roosevelt to join the Allied war effort in Europe but up to that time the United States would only help by economic means. Little did Roosevelt know that he would have no choice but to enter the war a few weeks later when the Japanese would bomb his fleet at Pearl Harbor. Perhaps if Roosevelt had gone along with Churchill earlier his fleet would have been on a war footing and made a better job of defending themselves when the Japanese attacked.

In 1940 an Allied Conference decided that we needed a minimum of forty battalions with full support to defend the Thai border alone, along with over 500 modern aircraft. There were in fact only around thirty-two battalions in Malaya and only about 150 aircraft, most of them obsolete, and no tanks at all to support the troops such as myself on the ground. When the Japanese invaded Thailand and Malaya on 7 December 1941, 6 Indian Infantry Brigade to which I was attached, bore the brunt of the onslaught at Jitra, Gurun and Kampar. Whilst many of the Indian troops in the division fought bravely, they were on the whole poorly trained, not familiar with the sight and sound of modern weapons and led by mainly inexperienced officers. Many of them defected to the Japanese after they had been captured, persuaded in most cases by an exiled Indian Nationalist called Pritam Sing. Sing had been recruited by the Japanese before the invasion and accompanied Colonel Saeki's troops as they advanced down Malaya. At Alor Star he was joined by a captured Punjabi officer Captain Mohan Sing, who even before the war had been stirring up anti British feelings within the Indian forces. Mohan Sing was now more than happy to co-operate with the Japanese and persuaded many of the vulnerable Indians to join them, on the strength that this would help liberate India from British rule.

I am convinced that my experiences during those dreadful four years have greatly influenced my thinking, my views on life in general and my attitudes towards my fellow man. Being held as a POW was in itself a life changing experience, but being on those two 'hell-ships' was simply the worst experience imaginable.

People often ask me if I am bitter about the grave mistakes made during those traumatic couple of months before Singapore fell. My reply has always been yes, not for myself but for the tens of thousands of my comrades who lost their lives either in battle, in POW camps or on those awful hell ships. I lost three and half years of my life but at least I was fortunate enough to come home.

I am very proud to have been with the East Surrey Regiment during those difficult years in Malaya, Singapore, Thailand and Japan, and well over sixty years later I still wear my regimental tie with pride. It deeply saddens me when I think that out of the 786 East Surreys who frolicked on the beaches of Penang during the summer of 1941, only 125 lived to see the green fields of their native England, Scotland, Ireland or Wales and their loved ones again. Around 516 men lost their lives during the battles in Malaya and in Singapore, with a further 125 dying of malnutrition, overwork and ill-treatment at the hands of the Japanese in prison camps and in the hell ships. Looking back all these years later, I am saddened by how our leaders managed to completely underestimate the capabilities of the Japanese, prior to the invasion of Malaya. *Time* magazine in its 30 December 1941 issue said of the Japanese:

> 'Big only in their fury. . .the little men, barefoot or wearing rubber sneakers, were advancing down Malaya on a miniature scale, using tiny one-man tanks and two-man gun carriers.'

The British even said that 'their doctors cut miniature Japanese bullets out of miniature British wounds.' This piece of fiction makes me laugh now, but we were not laughing at the time as we lay in a muddy trench near Kampar with full sized Japanese shells raining down on us. Major General Murray-Lyon was well aware of the capabilities and armaments of the Japanese and it is astonishing to think that folks back home were unaware of the full might of the military force we were facing.

Shortly after returning from captivity I attended a regimental reunion at the Chelsea Town Hall. The surviving Surreys were addressed by Colonel C.E. Morrison who told us, in an emotional speech, that a high-ranking Japanese commander in Bangkok had given orders to all camp commanders to dispose of the prisoners of war as they saw fit if the Japanese homeland was invaded by the Allies.

'This was to all intents and purposes a warrant for the massacre of all you men in this room along with many thousands of your comrades,' he said quietly.

As he paused, the hall was completely silent as the reality of his words sunk in and we all realised how lucky we had been.

A copy of the actual order was found in the safe in one of the camps in Japan after the war and is now in an archive in the US. I will just quote a small section:

'Under the current system, when you take refuge from bomb explosions you must make every prisoner being at one spot under strict caution and kill them all. Method: No matter individually, or in a group, by gas, by bomb, by poison, decapitated, be drowned, choose yourself which suits the occasion. The principle object is "leave no traces". Take every possible means for that.'

I have read many books about POWs held by the Japanese, but a paragraph in Hugh V. Clarke's book *Last Stop Nagasaki 1984* encapsulates all of my experiences poignantly:

'Being a POW was to become an involuntary subscriber to an extraordinary lottery. You could remain hungry and bored in Changi, but relatively undisturbed by your Japanese captors; you could work on the wharves and food dumps of Singapore and grow fat, if prepared to risk the inevitable bashings or worse; you could be shipped to Japan on the hell ships (allied subs permitting) and live in conditions worse than a Japanese miner or factory worker; or you could crack the bad luck jackpot and end up on the Burma – Siam railway.

I guess I cracked the bad luck jackpot, lost the throw of the dice several times over and still defied the odds to survive, for which I thank God.

More than sixty years on, the memories of those five and a half years spent in foreign fields are still fresh in my mind and on each VJ day that passes I feel a sense of pride that at least I did my best to defend the freedom of future generations.

We were all very aware during the spring of 1945, as we toiled ceaselessly in a stinking factory, that Japan was isolated economically from the rest of the world and it was just a matter of time before the end came. I was concerned that the end might come for me in a different way but, by the grace of God and good fortune, I survived and I'm certainly of the opinion that the dropping of the first atomic Bombs on Hiroshima and Nagasaki saved my life. Of course I regret the tragic loss of Japanese lives in those cities but it saved the lives of many Allied Prisoners of War and also the lives of many American and Japanese soldiers. Had the Americans invaded Japan in a conventional way then many more people would have died. President Harry Truman summed it up in his public statement to the American people shortly after the dropping of the first bomb on Hiroshima:

> 'We have used it against those who attacked us without warning at Pearl Harbor, against those who have starved, beaten and executed prisoners of war, against those who have abandoned all pretense of obeying international laws of warfare. We have used it in order to shorten the agony of the war. Nobody is more disturbed over the use of Atomic Bombs as I am but I was greatly disturbed over the unwarranted attack by the Japanese on Pearl Harbor and their murder of our prisoners of war.'

When the Americans began bombing Japanese cities in March 1945, the Japanese were told that the Allies were a totally 'bestial' enemy. They were never told about the bestiality *we* had to suffer at the hands of their military for three and a half years and this bit of hypocrisy has stuck firmly in the throats of most long suffering FEPOWs to this very day.

The House of Lords debated the fall of Singapore a few days after the capitulation and Lord Wedgwood delivered a most gloomy verdict when he said that: 'The surrender of Singapore is the blackest page in our military history for all time.' Wedgwood was most certainly right as British pride suffered a huge dent when the fall of Singapore turned out to be Britain's single most devastating event of the Second World War. At the time it was not for me, an ordinary young British conscript, to examine too closely the Japanese reasons for their struggle to dominate Asia, but today I still ask myself that very question – without finding an answer.

I am often asked what the worst parts of my experiences in the Far East were. With so many poignant memories I have always found it difficult to put them in any sort of order. But if I have to, my 'cruises' aboard the *Asaka Maru* and *Hakusan Maru* must be close to the top, closely followed by that fateful few hours in the Alexandra Military Hospital in Singapore, but really the whole experience was horrific.

After the war ended, the Captain of the *Asaka Maru*, Odake Bunji, was put on trial for war crimes and was found guilty of the ill-treatment of 750 British POWs, first aboard the *Asaka Maru* and later aboard the *Hakusan Maru*. The trial found him guilty of: overcrowding, inadequate sanitary conditions and living accommodation, lack of medical supplies and the provision of unsuitable food. All this resulted in the physical and mental suffering of many POWs and the death of others. I can certainly testify that these charges were indeed legitimate, and although I do not know what became of Bunji, I certainly hope that he paid the price for the suffering and hardships we endured on those hellish ships. Japanese figures after the war indicated that out of around 50,000 POWs shipped by sea to a variety of destinations during the war, some 10,800 died at sea – a terrible rate of over twenty per cent. Many died as a result of attacks by friendly fire from American submarines: others died of illness, diseases and starvation on board the stinking vessels. I suffered on land and again at sea during those two terrible voyages, but I was one of the lucky ones.

In 1985 I was reading the latest copy of the FEPOW News when I came across a letter from a Mrs Shaw asking if anyone knew about what had happened to her husband Tom, who had been killed during the Malaya/Singapore campaign. I was pretty sure that this was the same Spike Shaw who had been killed by the Sikh guard during our first few weeks in Changi POW camp. I contacted Mrs Shaw and told her that I might be able to give her some information about her late husband and arranged to visit her.

It was a very difficult and emotional moment as I told her the true facts about her husband's death. I explained to her that Tom, Spike and I were mates in Changi.

'He wasn't killed in action Mrs Shaw; he went over the wire with Tom to get a tin of milk and was shot by the Sikh guards,' I said.

She was most upset and it was a very emotional experience for me but at least she now knew the truth.

'It might have been much worse for him if he had gone on to work on the railway,' I said to try and ease the pain, but this was not much of a condolence.

'After all these years I now know the truth. Thank you John,' she said calmly.

By the laws of statistics I should not be here today telling you this story, but I firmly believe that someone somewhere was looking after me during those four years. Take a look at the odds that were stacked against me and you will appreciate why I believe this:

- During the conflict in Malaya and Singapore my regiment lost two thirds of its men.
- More than three hundred patients and staff in the Alexandra Military hospital were slaughtered by the Japanese.
- Twenty six percent of British soldiers slaving on the Burma/ Thai Railway died.
- More than fifty men out of around six hundred died aboard the *Asaka Maru* and the *Hakusan Maru*.
- Many more did not manage to survive the Japanese winter of 1944/45, the coldest winter in Japan since records began.

When I returned home people would often ask me what it was like to be free again. I experienced great difficulty in talking about my experiences to my family and friends but for some reason I had no difficulty in discussing the dreadful times with other POWs, perhaps because only they could really appreciate what I went through. The only words I could find to reply to such questions was only to thank God for looking after me and to say, 'Think to yourself: water is there at the turn of a tap, bread, butter, beans, milk, eggs, a cup of tea, an aspirin. Deprive yourself of them for even two or three weeks. Add in some bashings and a few deadly diseases. Take away your freedom to walk, talk and do what you like, when and where you like. Maybe you might just get a glimmer of what freedom means to me.' They would just nod their head in amazement.

It was one of the saddest moments of my life when Mick Shiels passed away in 1980 before we had the opportunity to meet up again.

I do keep in touch with Mick's widow Madeline and his brother Shaun, who lives not far away in New Malden. I probably owe my life to Mick as there were many occasions when I would certainly have given up if it had not been for his strength of will and positive approach to our situation. He was truly an inspirational man and I have dedicated this book to him.

Some years ago I came across this poignant verse in a magazine penned well over a century ago by an unknown old soldier. This perhaps sums up my feelings as I struggled to survive as a POW:

> *I asked God for strength, that I might achieve – I was made weak, that I might learn humbly to obey.*
> *I asked for help that I might do greater things – I was given infirmity, that I might do better things.*
> *I asked for riches, that I might be happy – I was given poverty, that I might be wise.*
> *I asked for all things, that I might enjoy life – I was given life, that I might enjoy all things.*
> *I got nothing that I asked for – but everything that I hoped for.*
> *Despite myself, my prayers were answered.*
> *I am among all men, most richly blessed.*

Despite the hardships in the Far East I truly believe that life has been very good to me. Perhaps my Roman Catholic faith has something to do with it; it was a great help to me during those dark years of despair as POW. I will end now with the words of the prayer I recited daily during those times of great hardship and suffering;

> *Jesus, Mary, Joseph I give you my heart and soul*
> *Mary conceived without sin pray for me*
> *Lord I am not worthy thou should enter under my roof*
> *Only save the world and I shall be saved.*
> *Amen*

John Wyatt

Appendix 1

Asaka Maru
Regulation for Prisoners

1. The prisoners disobeying the following orders will be punished with immediate death.
   (a) Those disobeying orders and instructions.
   (b) Those showing a motive of antagonism and raising a sign of opposition.
   (c) Those disobeying the regulations by individualism, egoism, thinking only about yourself, rushing for your goods.
   (d) Those talking without permission and raising loud voices.
   (e) Those walking and moving without order.
   (f) Those carrying unnecessary baggage in embarking.
   (g) Those resisting mutually.
   (h) Those touching the boat's materials, wires, electric lights, tools, switches etc.
   (i) Those climbing ladder without order.
   (j) Those showing action of running away from the room or boat.
   (k) Those trying to take more meal than given to them.
   (l) Those using more than two blankets.

2. Since the boat is not well-equipped and inside being narrow, food being scarce and poor you'll feel uncomfortable during the short time on the boat. Those loosing patience and disordering the regulation will be heavily punished for the reason of not being able to escort.

3. Be sure to finish your 'Nature's call' evacuate the bowels and urine before embarking.

4. Meal will be given twice a day. One plate only to one prisoner. The prisoners called by the guard will give out the meal quick as possible

and honestly. The remaining prisoners will stay in their places quietly and wait for your plate. Those moving from their places reaching for your plate without order will be heavily punished. Same orders will be applied in handling plates after meal.

5. Toilets will be fixed at the four corners of the room. The buckets and cans will be placed. When filled up a guard will appoint a prisoner. The prisoner called will take the buckets to the centre of the room. The buckets will be pulled up by the derrick and be thrown away. Toilet papers will be given. Everyone must co-operate to make the room sanitary. Those being careless will be punished.

6. Navy of the Great Japanese Empire will not try to punish you all with death. Those obeying all the rules and regulations and believing the action purposes of the Japanese Navy, co-operating with Japan in constructing the 'New order of the Great Asia' which lead to the world's peace will be well treated.

The End

Appendix 2

Japanese Surrender Document

INSTRUMENT OF SURRENDER OF JAPANESE FORCES UNDER THE COMMAND OR CONTROL OF THE SUPREME COMMANDER JAPANESE EXPEDITIONARY FORCES, SOUTHERN REGIONS, WITHIN THE OPERATIONAL THEATRE OF THE SUPREME ALLIED COMMANDER, SOUTH EAST ASIA

1. In pursuance of and in compliance with:

(a) the instrument of surrender signed by the Japanese plenipotentiaries by command and on behalf of the Emperor of Japan, the Japanese Government, and the Japanese Imperial General Headquarters at Tokyo on 2 September, 1945;
(b) general Order No. 1, promulgated at the same place and on the same date;
(c) the local agreement made by the Supreme Commander, Japanese Expeditionary Forces, Southern Regions, with the Supreme Allied Commander, South East Asia at Rangoon on 27 August 1945;

To all of which Instrument of Surrender, General Order and Local Agreement this present Instrument is complementary and which it in no way supersedes, the Supreme Commander Japanese Expeditionary Forces, Southern Regions (Field Marshal Tersuchi) does hereby surrender unconditionally to the Supreme Allied Commander, South East Asia (Admiral The Lord Louis Mountbatten) himself and all Japanese sea, ground, air and auxiliary forces under his command or control and within the operational theatre of the Supreme Allied Commander, South East Asia.

2. The Supreme Commander, Japanese Expeditionary Forces, Southern Regions, undertakes to ensure that all orders and instructions that may be issued from time to time by the Supreme Allied Commander, South East Asia, or by any of his subordinate Naval, Military or Air-Force Commanders of whatever rank acting in his name, are scrupulously and promptly obeyed by all Japanese sea, ground, air and auxiliary forces, Southern Regions, and within the operational theatre of the Supreme Allied Commander, South East Asia.

3. Any disobedience of, or delay or failure to comply with, orders or instructions issued by the Supreme Allied Commander, South East Asia, or issued on his behalf by any of his subordinate Naval, Military or Air-Force Commanders of whatever rank, and any action which the Supreme Allied Commander, South East Asia or his subordinate Commanders, acting on his behalf, may determine to be detrimental to the Allied Powers, will be dealt with as the Supreme Allied Commander, South East Asia may decide.

4. This instrument takes effect from the time and date of signing.

5. This instrument is drawn up in the English language, which is the only authentic version. In any case of doubt as to intention or meaning, the decision of the Supreme Allied Commander, South East Asia is final. It is the responsibility of the Supreme Commander, Japanese Expeditionary Forces, Southern Region, to make such translation into Japanese as he may require.

Signed at Singapore at 0341 hours (GMT) on 12 September, 1945.

Field Marshal Tersuchi Louis Mountbatten

Appendix 3

Buckingham Palace

The Queen and I bid you a very warm welcome home.

Through all the great trials and sufferings which you have undergone at the hands of the Japanese, you and your comrades have been constantly in our thoughts.

We know from the accounts we have already received how heavy those sufferings have been. We know also that these have been endured by you with the highest courage.

We mourn with you the deaths of so many of your gallant comrades.

With all our hearts, we hope that your return from captivity will bring you and your families a full measure of happiness, which you may long enjoy together.

George R.I.
September 1945

Appendix 4

From General Sir Richard Foster, KCB., C.M.G., D.S.O.
Colonel of the East Surrey Regiment,
Ladywell, Speen,
Newbury, Berks.

On behalf of everyone in the Regiment I send you the heartiest of welcomes; we are really delighted to think that you are back home. We know that our 2nd Battalion had a tremendous task to perform in the withdrawl of some 500 miles to Singapore; we also know that you acquitted yourselves nobly and maintained the fine tradition of the Battalion and the Regiment.

For over three and a half years you have been in the hands of a cruel and barbaric enemy and it has, perhaps, been difficult for us at home and those on other fronts to realise your hardships. None the less our thoughts, and I may add our prayers, have been with you all the time, and we thank God that you are back. There are, however, a number who can never return – we mourn their loss but they will not be forgotten.

Ever since the war with Japan started we made arrangements to send you out parcels of comforts and it has been heartbreaking that our brutal enemy prevented this succour.

That you may now enjoy peace and happiness is the wish of us all.
Yours sincerely

R. Foster

Bibliography

Abbott S, *And All My War is Done*, Pentland, Edinburgh, 1991.

Barber N, *Sinister Twilight*, Cassell, London, 1968.

Barwick, I. J, *In the Shadow of Death*, Pen & Sword, Barnsley, 2003.

Bayley C & Harper T, *Forgotten Armies*, Penguin, London, 2004.

Beattie R, *The Death Railway*, Image, Bangkok, 2005.

Braddon R, *The Naked Island*, Birlinn, Edinburgh, 2005.

Bradley J, *Towards the Setting Sun*, Fuller, Wellington NWS, 1982.

Bruton P, *British Military Hospital, Alexandra Singapore*, Bruton.

Chung OC, *Operation Matador*, Eastern University Press, Singapore, 2003.

Churchill W, *The Second World War*, Pimlico, London, 2002.

Clarke HV, *Last Stop Nagasaki*, Allen & Unwin, London, 1984.

Clarke HV, *A Life for Every Sleeper*, Allen & Unwin, Sydney, 1986.

Davies PN, *The Man behind the Bridge*, Athlone, London, 1991.

Daws G, *Prisoners of the Japanese*, Robson, London, 1995.

East Surrey Regiment, *The Final Years*.

East Surreys, *Malaya 1941 -1942*.

Farrell BP, *The Defence and Fall of Singapore 1940-1942*, Tempus, Stroud, 2003.

Hack K & Blackburn K, *Did Singapore Have to Fall*, Routledge, London, 2003.

Hastain P, *White Coolie*, Hodder & Stoughton, London, 1947.

Hastings M, *Nemesis*, Harper, London, 2007.

Horner RM, *Singapore Diary*, Spellmont, Stroud, 2007.

Kelly T, *Hurricane Over the Jungle*, Pen & Sword, Barnsley, 1984.

Kennedy J, *Andy Dillons Ill Fated Division*, United Writers, Cornwall, 2000.

Lane A, *Lesser Gods Greater Devils*, Lane, Stockport, 1993.

Lockwood SR, *Unbelievable But True*, Vanguard, Cambridge, 2006.

Loong CK, *The British Battalion in Malaya 1941-1942*.

Lomax E, *The Railway Man*, Cape, London, 1995.

Michno GF, *Death on the Hellships*, Leo Cooper, Barnsley, 2001.

Moffatt J & Holmes McCormack A, *Moon Over Malaya*, Tempus, Stroud, 2002.

MacArthur B, *Surviving the Sword*, Time Warner, London, 2005.

Mitchell R, *Baba Nonnie Goes to War*, Coombe, 2004.

Partridge J, *Alexandra Hospital Singapore*, Singapore Polytechnic, 1998.

Peek I.D, *One Fourteenth of an Elephant*, Transworld, London, 2004.

Russell Lord, *Knights of Bushido*, Corgi, London, 1960.

Saddington S, *Escape Impossible*, Lane, Stockport, 1997.

Searle R, *To the Kwai and Back*, Collins, London, 1986.

Skinner H, *Guest of the Imperial Japanese Army (1942-1945)*, Skinner, Littlehampton, 1993.

Smith C, *Singapore Burning*, Viking, London, 2005.

Summers J, *The Colonel of Tamarkan*, Simon & Schuster, London, 2005.

Thompson P, *The Battle for Singapore*, Piatkus, London, 2005.

Index